Describing Archival Materials:
The Use of the MARC
AMC Format

Describing Archival Materials: The Use of the MARC AMC Format

Richard P. Smiraglia
Editor

School of Library Service
Columbia University

The Haworth Press
New York • London

Describing Archival Materials: The Use of the MARC AMC Format has also been published as *Cataloging & Classification Quarterly*, Volume 11, Numbers 3/4 1990.

The Haworth Press, Inc. 10 Alice Street, Binghamton, NY 13904-1580
EUROSPAN/Haworth, 3 Henrietta Street, London WC2E 8LU England

Library of Congress Cataloging-in-Publication Data

Describing archival materials : the use of the MARC AMC format / Richard P. Smiraglia, editor.
    p. cm.
    Includes bibliographical references.
    ISBN 0-86656-916-2 (alk. paper)
    1. Cataloging of archival material — Data processing. 2. Cataloging of manuscripts — Data processing. 3. MARC System — United States — Format. I. Smiraglia, Richard P., 1952- .
Z699.5.A7D47 1990
025.3′0285 — dc20
                            90-43012
                                CIP

Describing Archival Materials: The Use of the MARC AMC Format

CONTENTS

ABOUT THE EDITOR

Richard P. Smiraglia, MLS, is Senior Lecturer in bibliographic control at the School of Library Service, Columbia University. Formerly Music Catalog Librarian of the University of Illinois at Urbana-Champaign, he is a frequent author and lecturer on music and nonbook material cataloging. He is currently conducting doctoral research at the University of Chicago on the implications of the use of bibliographic relationships to enhance the syndetic structure of the online catalog through authority control. Since the spring of 1988 he has been a faculty member of the Society of American Archivists' series of workshops on the use of library standards for archival description.

INTRODUCTION

New Promise for the Universal Control of Recorded Knowledge

Richard P. Smiraglia

This volume celebrates the increasing use and influence of the MARC format for Archives and Manuscripts Control (AMC). As the format and its inevitable companion, the online archival catalog, gain increasing acceptance among archivists, several major issues evolve. One is the adoption and adaptation of standards for archival control data; another is the acceptance of archival control techniques for use in library collections. The papers in this volume are addressed to a dual audience of library catalogers, who in order to make use of the archival control techniques embodied in the AMC format must gain familiarity with basic techniques of archival collections management, and archivists, who might need basic instruction in relevant library cataloging techniques.

Out of the accomplishments of pioneering archivists who already have built substantial archival databases in the major bibliographic utilities emerges once again the promise of the universal control of recorded knowledge. This tantalizing promise is the subject of this introduction, which explores traditions of archival and bibliographic cataloging and the theoretical context in which knowledge control operates, and the similarities and differences observed be-

1

tween archival and bibliographic materials. The concluding section recalls the origins of the dream of universal control of recorded knowledge, which creeps ever closer to reality, and suggests directions for future work that must take place in both archival and bibliographic communities if this goal is to be accomplished.

CATALOGING TRADITIONS, BIBLIOGRAPHIC AND ARCHIVAL

Not too long ago cataloging was the near-exclusive province of librarianship. A long tradition of bibliographic principles grew up around efforts to create catalogs of library collections (mostly books, but occasionally with equal treatment of non-book materials) that would facilitate recreational reading (listening, etc.), scholarship, research, etc., by providing access to individual items and works. An entirely separate, if not wholly different, tradition of archival principles was developed by archivists, who saw themselves as historians and keepers of unique records to facilitate historical scholarship. Not only did the two communities develop almost exclusive of one another, but they also developed seemingly very different sorts of retrieval tools with very different goals. Librarians had, by the end of the nineteenth century, begun to see themselves as partners in a network of sorts. If cataloging and catalogs could be standardized, two major benefits would result. First, the community could save both money and energy by sharing the bibliographic workload. The record of shared cataloging and attempts at union catalogs is plentiful, and although it was to be the 1970s that would see the technological victory of computerized shared networks, nevertheless it was clear from the beginning of the Library of Congress's card service in 1901 that great economy could be realized from the shared use of catalog data. Secondly, the library community (or at least the Anglo-American library community) realized that use of libraries could be facilitated through standardization. If a user could approach any catalog anywhere secure in the knowledge that the retrieval process would be the same (that is, that headings and classifications would be the same from institution to institution), then library use would be facilitated.[1]

The archival community developed catalogs in diversity. After all, archival materials are by definition unique; therefore all catalogs would likewise be unique — that is, there could be no sharing of control data. Also, whereas the library catalog was the major finding tool for library materials, the institutional archives catalog (if it existed at all) was often merely a first step in the retrieval process, not particularly pointing the way to individual items, but rather serving as an index to collections and their unique finding aids (indexes, registers, etc.).[2] Another source of tension or divergence within the archival community stems from the fact that what now may be referred to as the archival field has grown together out of what were somewhat separate traditions, historical manuscripts and public archives. Because the historical manuscripts repositories often were situated in libraries, and because in this tradition the focus was often on unique manuscript items, library techniques for bibliographic control often were utilized for the control of these manuscripts.[3]

As the 1990s open we find that the two traditions have come together to develop archival control as an equal partner in the cataloging process. The development of AMC in response to the desire of archivists to automate control of their collections has led to the implementation of automated cataloging programs. These programs have been carried out for the most part in the databases of the major bibliographic networks, where now archival collection data stand side by side with library catalog data. A movement to develop standards for archival data has yielded *Archives, Personal Papers, and Manuscripts (APPM)*,[4] now in its second edition, which is derived from the *Anglo-American Cataloguing Rules*, Second edition *(AACR2)*.[5] Attempts have been made to adapt *Library of Congress Subject Headings*[6] *(LCSH)* for archival use. A major advantage of these developments, of course, is that scholars can now find the records of both primary and secondary sources, as well as published material, in integrated files in the major bibliographic networks. As the use of AMC has grown, librarians have begun to learn that they too can control large collections of materials in archival fashion.

Although the archival and library communities remain distinctly separate and retain their own identities, automation has provided a bridge between the communities, and the long-awaited dream of universal control of recorded knowledge has for the first time become a real possibility. The techniques of archival control and bibliographic control also remain distinctly separate, but they can be seen to constitute parallel techniques for accomplishing the same goal — the universal control of recorded knowledge. In theoretical terms then, archival and bibliographic control are the same enterprise with the goal being to facilitate the best possible use of recorded knowledge, such use to be facilitated by a communicative retrieval process and common techniques for data creation, entry, and control.

A CONTINUUM: ARCHIVAL AND BIBLIOGRAPHIC CONTROL IN THEORY

To understand fully the thrust of the new archival control techniques, the reader must grasp both the underlying theory and the rationale for the differing practices of both the archival and bibliographic communities. The differing practices stem from one basic fact: archival materials are the raw stuff of recorded knowledge — the *records* of what has been done by whom, when, and under what circumstances. Published materials are the commercial result of an intellectual process. From this basic dilemma there stem three areas in knowledge control where differences are important: (1) physical differences in archival and bibliographic materials; (2) intellectual differences in archival and bibliographic entities; and, (3) theoretical differences in approach to retrieval of archival and bibliographic sources.

On the other hand, because archival and bibliographic control can be described as constituting the same enterprise with similar goals, there is a great deal of theoretical similarity between the two. That is: (1) there is not only a common goal, but also the objectives of control tools (catalogs and finding aids) are theoretically the same; (2) an intellectual-physical dichotomy in description is present in both archival and bibliographic control; and, (3) the problems inherent in any communicative information system are relevant to both.

This section will begin by describing knowledge control theory and then proceed to examine both major similarities and differences between archival and bibliographic control.

Knowledge Control: A Theoretical Context

The theoretical concepts that explain knowledge control have been described most eloquently by Patrick Wilson.[7] First, it is important to recognize that knowledge control is a process that includes the creation, storage, manipulation, and retrieval of data about knowledge artifacts. This process takes place in a conceptual space referred to as the universe of recorded knowledge, in which all instances of artifacts of recorded knowledge (books, journals, archives, paintings, etc.) are potential candidates for control and subsequent retrieval. Wilson's contribution is the notion that knowledge control operates in two domains, called the descriptive domain and the exploitative domain. The descriptive domain, which is repository-oriented, is the domain in which materials held by repositories are described (i.e., cataloged, indexed, etc.) in inherent terms to facilitate retrieval. The exploitative domain, which is user-oriented, is that domain in which information seekers are able not only to find, but also to exploit (i.e., make good use of) artifacts of recorded knowledge.

Clearly, both bibliographic and archival collections constitute potential descriptive domains. Catalogs and other finding aids are constructed according to basic descriptive principles, which utilize both inherent data from the materials (i.e., catalog descriptions), and abstracts (annotations, summaries, etc.), which are constructed to illuminate the inherent data by providing external data, based on the judgment of the compiler of the finding tool. The descriptive domain constitutes a precondition for the exploitative domain. That is, the ability of an information seeker to find and exploit recorded knowledge is dependent on the descriptive domain, wherein the knowledge artifacts have been described and ordered adequately in a finding tool.

Wilson's theoretical context, although presented in a forum devoted to bibliographic control, is universal and can be seen to embrace all efforts to control and retrieve recorded knowledge.

Major Similarities Between Archival and Bibliographic Control

Given the preceding framework of knowledge control, it becomes clear that both archival and bibliographic control exhibit theoretical similarities. Each has a common goal, which is accomplished with knowledge-control tools that have common objectives. The intellectual process of constructing the descriptive domain is plagued by a common physical-intellectual dichotomy. And a common dilemma exists in the construction of retrieval systems. These issues are explored below.

Common Goals and Objectives

First, the processes of archival and bibliographic control have a common goal, which is the exploitation of recorded knowledge. Because of the commonality represented by this goal, the unity of the two communities is coming about as both seek to contribute to the universal record of human knowledge. Herein lies our cause for optimism, for the long-held dream of universal control becomes ever more real as archives, and perhaps museums and other repositories of human endeavor, seek first to automate, then to integrate their finding tools with those of libraries.

The objectives of bibliographic and archival finding tools are the same; only their priority ranking differs. That is, the common objectives are: (1) to facilitate identification of specific items or intellectual entities; (2) to gather together sources produced by and about the same creator or in a single form; and, (3) to facilitate the evaluation of the data presented in the system by providing sufficient context. The objectives might be ranked differently for libraries and archives. The library traditionally has constructed a catalog that primarily facilitated identification, secondarily gathered together intellectual entities, and subsequently provided bibliographical context.[8] However, the archives traditionally has constructed a catalog that primarily gathered together intellectual entities, secondarily provided archival context, and only incidentally (because it is a low priority of information seekers) identified specific items. Even though the ranking of objectives differs and results in essentially different construction techniques for catalogs, still the objectives are identical and are all valid in each context.

A Common Descriptive Dichotomy

A physical-intellectual dichotomy is pervasive in the domain of descriptive control. That is, a cataloger must grapple with two properties of any material cataloged: (1) the physical properties, from which item (or collection) descriptions are derived; and, (2) the intellectual properties (i.e., the "work" or "intellectual content") from which access points are derived. In each case, the physical properties (e.g., titles, chronological designations, extent, etc.) are derived easily from the materials themselves and detailed in the catalog record. But the subsequent work of identifying, constructing, and controlling access points for intellectual entities is much more difficult. This process might involve little use of the described material. Rather, it is an intellectual process in which the cataloger must identify and label the creator(s) of an intellectual entity (the author of a book, the originator of archival records, etc.). Somehow these dichotomous data must be linked in the control tool to form a recognizable surrogate for the cataloged materials. Discussions of the concept of "main entry" (essential in one sense to identify an intellectual entity, but useless technologically in a properly constructed automated control system), are mired in this dichotomy.

Common Dilemma in Information Seeking

Michael Buckland describes the process of information-seeking as having three distinct stages: (1) inquiry formulation; (2) transformation of signals (from seeker to system as query, and from system to seeker as output); and, (3) exploitation of the information.[9] This presents the cataloging community with a communication dilemma. That is, the cataloger works from the materials (archival, bibliographic, etc.) with full knowledge of their content and form, and inputs data into the system. The information seeker works, from a curiosity or need, to formulate queries that must be transformed into the retrieval system's language, which has been input by the cataloger. But what guarantee is there that the cataloger, who is looking at the objects, will formulate system language that is accessible by information seekers, or that information seekers, who do not know what is contained in the system but have a vague idea of what is sought, will choose language that matches that input by the cataloger? This dilemma is pervasive in the knowledge control community, for the battle between the cataloger and information seeker must always be fought, with eternally uncertain results.

Major Differences Between Archival and Bibliographic Control

Despite the theoretical commonalities between archival and bibliographic control, traditional differences in the techniques used to accomplish control arise from fundamental differences such as: (1) the physical characteristics of the materials; (2) the intellectual differences that stem from different creative origins; and, (3) differences in information seeking behavior. These differences will be explored briefly below.

Physical Differences

The physical differences between the materials held by archives (predominantly primary sources) and those held by libraries (predominantly secondary sources) are obvious. Primary sources are records produced in conjunction with the conduct of some activity, whether administrative or personal. Because such sources are not created to facilitate knowledge retrieval, they have no deliberate structure in a bibliographic sense. That is, they do not have title pages, colophons, copyright notices, etc. — the usual sources of inherent descriptive data. Published materials, on the other hand, are deliberately produced for consumption, often with some commercial motivation. There is a centuries-old tradition of book publishing from which most bibliographic descriptive standards are derived. Books have formal sources of inherent descriptive data (those listed above as lacking from primary sources, and more, such as indexes, source attributions, etc.). In many cases, even unpublished secondary sources display many of these characteristics as well, so pervasive is the influence of the book format.

Thus the physical differences between archival and bibliographic materials are great, because published materials have a long history of relative standardization of form and substance, while archival collections can include anything (and often do), in no particular prescribed organizational format. The whole tradition of library cataloging is derived from a tradition of bibliography that respects the sanctity of the published item's inherent bibliographic characteristics. Thus the name of a book is its title, and published works are cited uniformly by using the combination of the name of the creator (author, composer, etc.) and the title as found on the title page.

How then, should an archival collection be described? It has no inherent archival characteristics because it was not collected and organized by its creator for the purpose of being deposited in an archive. Rather, the materials are the raw stuff of creation — correspondence, notes, financial records, photographs, etc. — organized as they were created in whatever way best suited the needs of the creator. There is no chief source of information, there are no statements of responsibility, there are no copyright notices or statements about manufacture or distribution; in other words, there is no reliable archival component that could serve as a parallel to a bibliographic chief source of information. Relying on the notion that finding aids compiled by the archival repository will serve as useful aids to archival retrieval, archival cataloging as dictated by the current standards relies on formal finding aids (registers, lists, indexes, etc.) to supply collection titles, historical scope notes, and such other information as is considered useful for retrieval.

Intellectual Differences

Intellectual differences between archival and bibliographic materials also must be contemplated. Published materials usually are created in a definitive or at least purposive manner by some person or corporate entity. Further, published materials are usually clearly about something — for as Wilson reminds us, no one can write something without knowing what he writes about (and one supposes that even works of art — musical performances, sculpture, painting, etc. — are created with a definite message in the creator's mind).[10]

Archival materials, by contrast, are not always clearly "by" or "about" anything. Schellenberg says that "records are created and accumulated to accomplish certain functions, activities, or transactions. If they deal with subjects, it is because the subjects are the object of action."[11] The creator is the person or body who has caused the materials to be gathered. Thus an archival collection of correspondence might contain only letters received by the person. Obviously the letters are not by the person, but surely the collection of them is. Then, too, are the letters "about" the recipient? Probably not directly so, in the sense that a biography is about the biographee. But can't a scholar learn something about a subject by perusing the correspondence received by that person? So in some sense the collection of letters is in its entirety about the recipient.

The intellectual difference can be summarized as the difference between works that are created deliberately (histories, novels, operas, etc.), and records of some activity that are accumulated to accomplish that activity. Any published work is viewed as the product of the forces that created it, and anything it contains can be cited definitively as the result of those forces. Archival materials are the sources that can be used to create such definitive works. But in and of themselves their content is more subjective, or intuitive, or perhaps inferential, than the processed and carefully constructed content of any published work. To the archival cataloger this means that the otherwise carefully delineated concepts of "by" and "about" are confused and perhaps even equivalent.

Information-Seeking Differences

As a consequence, the theoretical perspective on retrieval also is affected, because archival and published materials will be used in different ways, and therefore they might be sought in different ways. The seeker of bibliographic material is likely to know something specific about the items or works that will be sought in the system. So a fundamental of bibliographic control is the identification of known items and works. Even subject searching to some extent is dependent on what is known by the seeker about the materials. Archival materials, because their use might be more inferential, also might tend to be sought in ways that are more inferential; thus archivists rely heavily on extended reference interviews to assist information seekers, and finding tools are a secondary consideration. The scholar might know that a certain set of records is held by a specific repository, and that there is a probability that in those records useful information might be found. But the known-item search is not thought to be a common approach to archival records, and therefore archival catalogs have not depended so heavily on transcribed characteristics for known-item identification, and they must have depended more heavily on indexing techniques that could facilitate inferential searching. As a result, archival descriptions rely little on traditional bibliographic elements, such as titles, and heavily on notes, such as those that provide historical contextual information, detail the scope of the records, and outline the organizational structure of the collection.[12]

PAPERS IN THIS VOLUME

The papers in this volume present the techniques of archival control in the order in which they must be applied. All of the papers are essentially pragmatic, though each author grapples with relevant aspects of the issues outlined above. Each paper, where appropriate, contains examples of AMC records to illustrate the various techniques.

The volume opens with a paper by Michael Fox detailing the requisite details of archival description, including the construction of finding aids, and the representation of archival collections in catalogs according to the recognized standard, *APPM*. Fox also notes the central concepts of archival organization, which ultimately determine the construct of finding tools, and explains the distinction between the terms "library cataloging" and "archival description." These are the concepts of provenance and original order, which essentially dictate that the materials retain information value only in the context in which their creator held them.

Edward Swanson's paper on choice and form of access points builds on the concepts presented by Fox. Swanson discusses concepts of intellectual responsibility, wherein the provenance is seen to constitute the act of creation (an analog to the authorship concept in bibliographic control), and the basic concepts of choice and formulation of access points, derived directly from *AACR2*. Access points representing subjects are considered by Richard Smiraglia, who provides an archival translation of basic indexing concepts such as subject analysis and indexing depth, all within the context of *LCSH*, which has been adapted for use as a technique of archival description. Marion Matters then takes up the concepts of authority control of both names and subjects, considering problems of both file management (or the actual "control" of headings) and potential for increased syndetic depth in archival contexts that can be provided if authority control as we now understand it is broadened.

The AMC format has been the catalyst for this burgeoning unity of archival and bibliographic control. Lisa Weber, who played instrumental roles in both the construction of the format and the education of archivists about it, outlines the design issues that contributed to the construction of the format, most of which are results of the differences and similarities discussed above, and then proceeds to detail the appropriate method of content designation for archival descriptions. A contribution by Kathleen Roe discusses the development of local archival automation by further detailing the requirements of archival information systems, in particular focusing on archival management features, and problems inherent in attempts to design systems that integrate archival and bibliographic records.

Because the basic principles and techniques that are presented in the preceding papers all describe the control of textual materials, a field for which standards have been developed, the three papers that make up the final section examine the archival control of nontextual materials, a burgeoning field attempting to derive standards from those for textual materials in a manner similar to that in which library standards for bibliographic control of nonbook materials were derived in the 1950s and 1960s from the century-old techniques for bibliographic control of books. This section opens with a paper by Barbara Orbach in which the value of archival visual images (photographs and films, etc.) provides a central focus. Orbach also provides a detailed look at the many standards that have been developed for the description of visual materials. Providing a contrast is a paper by David Thomas, in which the problems of collecting and describing archival collections of sound recordings are detailed. Thomas focuses his discussion around the concept of sound as an archival entity and the necessary adaptation of techniques of archival description for materials for which no standards exist. This adaptation requires the blending of techniques for archival description with techniques for bibliographic control of sound recordings, two traditions that are often fundamentally opposed. In the third paper by James Corsaro, the archival control of cartographic materials and the beginning of efforts to develop standards are discussed. While these final papers are by no means universal in their coverage of nontextual materials, in that many other kinds of nontextual materials are also treated archivally, they are representative, in that they detail the different considerations that apply to nontextual archival materials and the needs that must be considered in the construction of descriptive standards.

CONCLUSION

In the context of bibliographic control theory, there appear to be no theoretical differences between the goals and objectives of archival and bibliographic control. However, there are great differences in the details of physical and intellectual properties of materials, descriptive techniques, and system design considerations.

The challenge for the future is to continue cooperative efforts to develop universal knowledge control, to realize the dream first presented to the bibliographic community by Paul Otlet and Henri La Fontaine in the nineteenth century. In 1895 Otlet and La Fontaine founded the International Institute of Bibliography, one aim of which was to create a universal catalog that would exercise bibliographic control over the entire spectrum of recorded knowledge. Much of the modern field of library and information science owes its origins to this early attempt to compile a central record of all documentary knowledge. Like many other attempts to create union catalogs, Otlet and La Fontaine's movement foundered on both the primitive manual technology that could not adequately support the effort and on various national and international political difficulties.[13]

Now, near the end of the twentieth century, online bibliographic networks (finally facilitated by computer technology and rapidly growing in scope, both in types of knowledge artifacts controlled and in the international spread of contributed holdings) have begun to make Otlet and La Fontaine's dream a reality. This innovation of automation of knowledge control has shown many intellectual communities the pathway to universal control. And automation has been a catalyst for innovations in all documentary communities, most recently in the archival community. The result of cooperation among the bibliographic and archival communities might well be the attainment of a long-held dream.

In the not-too-distant future both communities must face three challenges. First, knowledge-control retrieval systems must be redesigned so that they no longer represent automated card files, but instead make efficient use of relational database designs. Second, the expansion of authority control to embrace the coexistence of authorship, provenance, form, genre, occupation, and provenance must take place to facilitate the further integration of automated records for all materials. Finally, standards must be developed that facilitate the common construction of descriptions for nontextual materials, and broaden the scope of subject and form thesauri. These might appear to be very pragmatic objectives, but in fact their attainment will require a thorough rethinking of much of the theoretical framework of knowledge control. These efforts are essential to the management of archival repositories as well as of libraries. Their results will be a continued enhancement of the quality of human life.

NOTES

1. For a detailed examination of the convergence of cooperative cataloging efforts at the end of the 19th century, see Kathryn Luther Henderson, "'Treated With A Degree of Uniformity and Common Sense': Descriptive Cataloging in the United States, 1876-1976." *Library Trends* 25 (1976): 227-271.

2. Archivists have been urged to review the history and techniques of library cataloging. For an interesting chronological comparison of the development of these separate traditions see T. R. Schellenberg, "Part I: Development of Principles and Techniques" in *The Management of Archives*. (New York and London: Columbia University Press, 1965), [1]-63.

3. For historical explanation of this divergence see Richard C. Berner, *Archival Theory and Practice in the United States: A Historical Analysis*. (Seattle and

London: University of Washington Press, 1983). For an overview of institutional tensions see William J. Maher, "Improving Archives-Library Relations: User-Centered Solutions to a Sibling Rivalry." *Journal of Academic Librarianship* 15 (Jan. 1990): 355-363.

4. *Archives, Personal Papers, and Manuscripts*. 2nd ed. (Chicago: Society of American Archivists, 1989).

5. *Anglo-American Cataloguing Rules*, 2nd ed., 1988 Revision. (Chicago: American Library Association, 1988).

6. Library of Congress, Subject Cataloging Division, *Library of Congress Subject Headings*. 13th ed. (Washington, DC: Library of Congress, Cataloging Distribution Service, 1990).

7. Patrick Wilson, *Two Kinds of Power: An Essay on Bibliographical Control*. (Berkeley: University of California Press, 1968).

8. This ranking of objectives is traditional, but it has been seriously questioned, most recently by Patrick Wilson. See his "The Second Objective." In *The Conceptual Foundations of Descriptive Cataloging*. Ed. by Elaine Svenonius. (San Diego: Academic Press, 1989), pp. 5-16; and "Interpreting the Second Objective of the Catalog." *Library Quarterly* 59 (1989): 339-353.

9. Michael Buckland, "Chapter 8: Retrieval," in *Library Services in Theory and Context*. 2nd ed. (Oxford: Pergamon Press, 1988), pp. 82-114.

10. Patrick Wilson, "Chapter V: Subjects and the Sense of Position." In *Two Kinds of Power*, pp. 69-92.

11. Schellenberg, *Management of Archives*, p. 68.

12. Like library bibliographic control, little is actually known about the ways in which users of archives seek information. Since the introduction of automated systems the archival profession has begun to examine this problem. Recent papers hint that known-item searching might actually be taking place more often than was previously suspected. For an overview see Lawrence Dowler, "The Role of Use in Defining Archival Practice and Principles: A Research Agenda for the Availability and Use of Records." *American Archivist* 51 (Winter and Spring, 1988): 74-86.

13. See W. Boyd Rayward, "The Evolution of an International Library and Bibliographic Community." *Journal of Library History* 16 (1981): 449-452; and *The Universe of Information: The Work of Paul Otlet for Documentation and International Organisation*, Federation International de Documentation Publication no. 520. (Moscow: VINITI, 1975).

Descriptive Cataloging
for Archival Materials

Michael J. Fox

SUMMARY. This paper describes the significant characteristics of archival materials and of archival methods of description and arrangement. Key sections of *Archives, Personal Papers, and Manuscripts* are explicated with particular reference to the ways in which this code reflects the nature of contemporary archival records and practice while remaining compatible with the style and structure of bibliographically oriented cataloging. The relationship of catalog records to other forms of archival finding aids is explained.

The effort to organize, describe and make accessible a body of materials is a common cause of librarians, archivists, curators and other information professionals. The approaches used by each group vary with the nature of the materials and the traditions and purposes of those who manage them. This article is an attempt to explain the archival approach to descriptive cataloging with particular reference to the parallels to and compatibility with its library counterpart.

THE NATURE OF DESCRIPTION

The descriptive catalog record stands as a surrogate for a tangible cultural entity — a published monograph, a videorecording, a manuscript collection, a three-dimensional object. The types of information that must be included to make a description useful vary for the

Michael J. Fox is Head of Processing, Division of Library and Archives at the Minnesota Historical Society, St. Paul, MN 55101. He currently represents the Society of American Archivists on ALCTS' Committee on Cataloging: Description and Access.

different categories of materials being cataloged. The details that characterize and therefore are used to identify a particular edition of *Moby Dick* differ from those necessary to describe the software product *WordPerfect 5.0*. Decisions about what to include in the record are derived from an understanding of the nature of the materials themselves rather than from abstract concepts. What features define a videorecording and distinguish one recording from another or from a piece of computer software? Our response reflects the practical need of the cataloger to meet the twin requirements of identification and differentiation.

Sometimes these cataloging variations simply reflect the unique physical characteristics of a class of materials: encoding format, recording speed, tape density, etc. In other cases, there are more fundamental differences in the basic intellectual description of the object. For a published work, it is bibliographic information — title, statements of responsibility, imprint, etc. — that largely defines the object. The details of its publication as a single, discrete item define its cultural context. These data elements are transcribed by the cataloger from closely prescribed portions of the work itself to create the description.

For a collection of materials organized according to archival principles, cultural context is defined by the collection's provenance, or source, rather than by publication data. Here, intellectual description centers on the title and on explanatory notes about such matters as the material's origin, organization, arrangement, scope, and content. These are supplied by the cataloger based on the "interpretation, extraction, and interpolation"[1] of information from various sources. Though bibliographic and archival records are each derived in a different manner, both serve the same surrogate role, conveying to the reader an understanding of the nature of the original.

Fortunately, there are common elements that permit us to integrate these different types of descriptions into one catalog. While varying in details, all include two basic elements: an intellectual characterization and a physical description of the item. Common stylistic conventions for presentation further unify the records. Finally, the use of uniformly constructed access points makes it possible to retrieve descriptions of materials that differ in their physical and intellectual properties. In such an integrated catalog, all related materials may be reached through a single search. Access to collections is not arbitrarily compartmentalized and scattered by physical format.

The following discussion reviews the principal elements of descriptive cataloging for archival materials, emphasizing the ways in which that practice reflects the nature of the materials. It ends with a brief explanation of the place of catalog records in the overall system of descriptive finding aids that might be found in a typical archival repository. First, a bit of archival theory and vocabulary.

THE NATURE OF ARCHIVES

Archival materials appear in many forms and originate from different sources. They include collections of personal papers organized around an individual or family as well as single, handwritten or typescript pieces such as diaries, letters, or speeches. Both are sometimes collectively referred to as manuscripts so as to distinguish them from archives, the corporate records of private organizations and government bodies. In this paper, the terms archives and archival embrace all three categories.[2] Unless otherwise qualified, characteristics ascribed to collections apply equally to those of personal papers and corporate records.

Archives are not defined by their physical medium, like videorecordings, or by the condition of their issuance, like serials, but rather by the principles of respect for provenance and original order by which they are described and physically organized. In a sense, it is the way in which they are handled by their custodian that makes them archival. The following properties are typical of archives.

— *Collections rather than individual items are the units of intellectual analysis.* A collection consists of materials that have come together in the natural course of some human activity. For individuals, these may be documents like those created or accumulated by Meridel Le Sueur in the course of her activities as an author, feminist, and political activist. When gathered together, they become the Meridel Le Sueur Papers. For a corporate body, such as a state Department of Corrections, the analog to a collection is the record group, comprising all the documentation created by that organization to meet its daily managerial, custodial, and correctional responsibilities. In both instances, it is a common provenance that binds the material together into a coherent, identifiable unit.

— *Collections may be physically and intellectually subdivided.* The most common subunit is the series, a group of materials related by creation, use, form, or receipt. Within the records of the aforementioned state Department of Corrections, there is probably a separate file folder containing documents on each inmate. Collectively, these files form a record series by virtue of their common contents, use, and arrangement and storage within the office, a series perhaps known as the Inmate Case Files. For ease of presentation, statements in this paper relating to "collections" are meant to apply equally to manuscript collections, to archival record groups, and to series.

— *Catalog descriptions may be created for any level of this hierarchy: for the entire collection, for a series within it, for a particular file unit such as individual inmate case file, or even for a single piece therein.* Entries in the national databases today typically describe government records at the series level and personal papers at the collection level. Sometimes, of course, an entire collection might consist of a single diary, letter, minute book, etc., which is individually described.

— *Because collections grow organically from the activities, lives and actions of organizations and individuals, the archivist must respect and preserve such provenance.* The contents of the records are intrinsically bound up with and cannot be fully understood apart from the life of the individual or functions of the organization from which they emanated. Who was this person? What was the nature of this organization? What was the governmental function that produced these files? Provenance provides the cultural context in which the records become intelligible and serves as a key descriptive element. As an exception to this principle, the archivist might occasionally create an artificial collection that draws together disparate items having a common theme, subject or format for purposes of better physical control or intellectual access.

— *The organic origin of archives also affects their physical arrangement and organization.* In contrast to a published work, which presents the cataloger with a fixed internal structure, the archivist is frequently faced with the necessity of determining a proper internal order and arrangement for items in a newly-received collection. Here the guiding principle is respect for and retention of their original order since this reflects the way the records were created and used. When materials are severely disorganized, the cataloger attempts to reconstruct a rational order which is sensitive to the nature and uses of the materials. Because they were initially assembled for purposes other than research in an archival institution, collections might require other physical processing in order to be rendered usable by researchers. This includes weeding of extraneous items, basic conservation work, and repackaging into permanent folders and boxes.[3]

—A collection might contain items in only a single physical format or many. It might consist entirely of computer files, photographs, or textual materials or include some of each. Collections are not media specific though this discussion focuses on those that include only "language materials" or are of mixed media.

—Each collection is unique. While certain pieces therein might exist in multiple copies, the corpus of each collection and its cataloging is unique. Except for reproductions and a few situations in which different institutions hold very similar records, shared cataloging is not a practical consideration.

—Most collections lack the formal elements of publication such as title pages, statements of authorship, and details of imprint. Description is not a matter of creating authoritative records for shared cataloging but rather the formulation of intelligible explanations for users who might be totally unfamiliar with the content, nature and structure of primary source material.

—The catalog record is a basic component in the system of descriptive finding aids but certainly not the only one used in most archival institutions. It serves as an introduction and pointer to other descriptive tools. Collections that are physically very large and varied in content and format require more detailed description than can be provided to the reader in a catalog entry. Registers, inventories, indexes, and calendars are prepared to meet this need.

AACR2 AND APPM

Though chapter four of the *Anglo-American Cataloguing Rules*, second edition[4] (*AACR2*) provides conventions for the description of archival materials, it has not been widely employed by archivists. Oriented to the cataloging of individual manuscripts, it fails to provide guidance for handling collections. The appearance in 1983 of *Archives, Personal Papers and Manuscripts* (*APPM*), compiled by Steven L. Hensen, then of the Library of Congress, provided an alternative that was more consistent with contemporary archival practice and compatible with library description in other areas.[5] Since then, it has become the de facto standard for archival descriptive cataloging. A second, expanded edition appeared in 1989.[6] This work parallels several others produced by LC and ALA to provide supplementary rules for describing specialized materials,[7] as anticipated in *AACR2* under rule 0.1.[8]

Figure 1, which is an imaginary record, was created according to the principles defined in chapter one of *APPM*. It illustrates some of the unique and significant features of that code which are explicated in the following sections. See references within the text refer to the relevant chapters in *APPM*.

CHIEF SOURCE OF INFORMATION

Since archival collections lack a consistent physical structure and presentation, the sources of descriptive information must be more broadly construed than with published works. The chief sources are, in the order of preference, the finding aid prepared for the collection, provenance and accession records, the materials themselves, and reference sources. For individual items, the piece itself is the chief source (see 1.0B1). One practical consequence is that, except for probable or uncertain dates, brackets will not be found in archival descriptions.

Title

The cataloger will occasionally encounter a formal title in a caption, header, or on a title page. In these cases, titles and statements of responsibility are transcribed according to the familiar rubric:

"exactly as to wording, order and spelling but not necessarily as to punctuation or capitalization"[10] (see 1.1B1). Other title information and edition statements are also rendered according to familiar principles (see 1.1E, 1.2). Signatures on individual pieces of correspondence are not considered to be statements of responsibility (see 1.1F).

In most cases, the cataloger must formulate a title for the collection, one that both describes and uniquely identifies it. Supplied titles are built around the following elements.

The basic component is a term that specifies the form or forms of material found in the collection. For individual textual items, the "most specific and appropriate" phrase is used, such as diary, journal, letterpress book, account book, or minute book. For collections consisting entirely of a single type of material, the plural form of the term is used, e.g., letters, photographs, legal documents. Where two forms of material are included, both may be given in the title, e.g., "Letter and map."

By convention, when a collection contains more than two types of material, the generic term "Papers" is assigned to groups of personal papers, and "Records" to the archives of corporate bodies. "Collection" or "Collection of papers" is used for groupings that have been artificially assembled around an individual, topic, or activity. Other data may be included in the title to provide further clarification. The name of the individual or organization around whom the records were created may be added optionally, as in the "Alexander Hamilton papers," the "Holman Municipal Airport records," or the "Allyn Kellogg Ford collection." This element is often omitted if the name is equivalent to the main entry. The decision to include or omit it might affect the way in which the collection will be cited. A preferred citation note later in the record can clarify this matter. Additional language describing the purpose, function, subject matter, or origins of the collection may be added to provide more identification, such as "Unemployment compensation case files" or "California travel diaries" (see 1.1B4).

The final title element is the date, included here since there is no imprint. For single pieces, exact dates are given in the form—year, month, day. Since a collection typically spans a range of time, the inclusive dates of the materials are given. In some circumstances,

Figure 1

Provenance, William Fonds, 1897-1956.

Papers, 1917-1955 (bulk 1925-1937).

15.4 cubic ft. (15 boxes and 1 partial box).

Diaries: 36 v.

Diaries: 2 microfilm reels; 35 mm.

Archivist and literary critic. Born at Last Chance, Nevada,
January 4, 1897. Served in World War I as an ambulance driver.
Graduated from Freen College in 1924 with a degree in cryp-
togamic botany. Following a career as a literary critic for
various French magazines, developed his epic work Quarks: the
Tao of Archives. Died March 15, 1956 in Frostbite Falls, Minn.

Correspondence relating chiefly to Provenance's career as a literary critic, plus diaries (1935-1937) and research notes pertaining to his development of the quark theory of archival description. Principle correspondents include Sigmund Freud, Ernest Hemingway, and Theodore Schellenberg as well as other prominent literary figures and archivists.

Diaries also available on microfilm.

Organized into four series: I. War Participation, 1917-1919; II. College Years, 1920-1924; III. European Career, 1925-1932; IV. Archival Career, 1933-1952.

Gift of Gertrude Provenance Thruxton.

Until 2010, quotation or publication of anything in or based on the collection requires written permission of the donor.

Inventory available in repository.

25

these are misleading since the majority of the collection might fall within a narrower time frame. The cataloger may bring that fact to the reader's attention by the addition in parentheses of bulk dates, in this manner: Papers, 1875-1965 (bulk 1890-1927) (see 1.1B5).

Descriptive notes usually follow the physical description. Since they are so integral a part of the intellectual description of archival materials, they will be considered next, though "out of order."

Notes

Judging from what has been said about the nature of archives, the information provided in the record up to this point would not give the reader an adequate understanding. Descriptive notes are essential for conveying a full sense of the origins, content, and structure of the materials. Indeed, they are the heart of the record. *APPM* provides guidance on the structure of and dictates a prescribed order for seventeen notes that are most likely to be used in archival cataloging. In style, most are presented as full sentences rather than in the concise and structured style that often characterizes note writing. Several can become rather lengthy. To improve comprehensibility, they may be broken into two or more paragraphs. The use and format of several of these notes will benefit from a brief explanation.

Biographical/Historical Note

Since collections are assembled around the life or activities of an individual or corporate body, key biographical details or historical data about the organization are essential to place the material in the proper context. However, as Hensen clearly points out, information should be limited to that which is relevant to the collection's contents. A common practice has developed in which this note is divided into two parts: an introductory, summary statement and its elaboration in the following sentence(s). This convention arises from a desire to be able to extract a shorter version of this note for inclusion in a printed repository guide or for a briefer display in an online catalog. The first sentence is written to stand alone and meet that need (see 1.7B1).

Scope and Content/Abstract Note

Arguably the most important part of the record, this note provides a narrative description of the "general contents, nature and scope" of the collection. It typically begins with an enumeration of the various forms of material found in the collection, such as papers, diaries, maps, journals, case files, etc. This is followed by an explanation of the functions and activities that generated the records and an enumeration of the most important persons, events, topics and places represented therein. The cataloger should also note things which one might expect to be included but which are absent as well as unusual things one might not expect to find. The names of important correspondents or general terms that characterize those individuals, e.g., "includes correspondence with leading British playwrights and actors" may be included. This note often provides the link between the description and the various names and terms assigned as access points to the collection. As in the biographical note, the first sentence may be constructed to provide a summation, a topical sentence capable of standing alone, followed by a more detailed elaboration (see 1.7B2).

Linking Entry Complexity Note

It is possible to catalog all or any portion of a collection. The description of any component part is tied to the next larger unit in the collection through a linking entry note, placing that subunit in its proper hierarchical context. For example, a series like the "Mayoral Subject Files" is linked to its parent collection, the Hubert Humphrey Papers. Such a description of a part within a whole is equivalent to the concept of "In" analytics. The citation in this note is introduced by an appropriate linking phrase. If the catalog record at hand describes a group of materials, such as a series within a larger collection, the reference begins with the phrase "Forms part of," e.g., "Forms part of: Humphrey, Hubert H. (Hubert Horatio), 1911-1978. Papers, 1919-1978." If the record is for an individual item, use "In," e.g., "In: Holman Municipal Airport. Records, 1927-1945" (see 1.7B3).

Microfilm and Other Reproductions

The description of microforms and other reproductions of archival materials is a complex problem. One encounters numerous permutations. Part or all of a collection might be on film. The originals might be held by the cataloging institution, another organization, a private party, or might have been discarded. The film might have been produced by the repository or by the original custodian. It might have been done for preservation, for bulk reduction, as part of an ongoing records management program, produced at the request of a single patron, or as a formal microfilm publication. It might be available for sale or only for use in the repository. One must decide whether the descriptive solution will be bibliographic or archival. Will the reproduction be cataloged separately, as an original publication or a reproduction, or is it part of an archival collection? Hensen indicates that the answer "will depend on the purposes of the catalog and the needs of the repository for more or less detail and content analysis. . . ."[11] Three notes are presented that provide guidance but not definitive solutions. As always, these notes are used in conjunction with information in the physical description area.

If the answer is a separate bibliographic record for the microfilm, proceed in accordance with chapter 11 of the Anglo-American Cataloguing Rules[12] and the relevant Library of Congress rule interpretations.[13] Consider the following common scenarios when treating film archivally. When the institution holds both the originals and reproductions of all or part of them, both media are included in the physical description. An Additional Physical Form Available Note (see 1.7B4) describes that which is available on microfilm. When one holds a portion of the collection in the original and other parts only in microform, their originals being elsewhere or no longer extant, both are mentioned in the physical description. If the originals have been destroyed, convey that information in a Reproduction Note (see 1.7B5). If they are elsewhere, record the name and address of the other repository in a Location of Originals/Duplicates Note. As the name suggests, this latter note may also be used to record the names of other institutions having reproductions of the work at hand (see 1.7B6).

Organization and Arrangement Note

The structure and order of items within the collection might not be readily apparent, but can be significant to the user. For example, land deeds that are arranged by parcel number will be unusable unless the number is known. This note conveys information about two concepts. Organization is the manner in which the collection as a whole is divided into smaller units. Arrangement describes the pattern (alphabetical, chronological, numerical) in which materials are ordered with a particular portion of the unit, e.g., "Case files arranged chronologically by date of admission."

Arrangements that are implied by the nature of the materials, e.g., that a diary is kept chronologically, need not be noted. Various portions of a collection may be arranged in different ways. The correspondence is filed alphabetically; subject files are ordered by topic. When relationships are complex, it might be necessary to divide this information into two or more notes for clarity of presentation (see 1.7B7).

Two related and sometimes confused notes are used to describe the history of materials prior to their entry into the repository.

Provenance Note

At times it might be useful to provide relevant details on the history of the custody of the materials prior to the time of their acquisition, e.g., previous ownership by another institution, information about collectors, or details about the chain of ownership (see 1.7B9).

Immediate Source of Acquisition Note

Here one lists the donor or other source of the material and such details as date, method of acquisition (donation, purchase, transfer), price, and accession number. Depending on the nature of the materials and the terms of the transaction by which it was acquired, one might wish either to prominently mention or suppress the public display of such data. It can also be viewed as collection management information, useful for administrative control rather than description. Its utility for that purpose might depend on the availability, existing or anticipated, of an automated management support system, which records and tracks internal operations such as the solicition of donations (see 1.7B10).

Another pair of notes have been defined to deal with two related problems often encountered with regard to access to archival collections.

Restrictions on Access Note

Restrictions on access come from many sources. Permission to use the materials might be controlled by statute — a state archives has collected vital records that may not be used for 75 years. Some materials may only be seen by certain authorized classes of person, e.g., student transcripts. The archivist might be required to restrict access to personal papers for a given period of time or at the donor's discretion under the terms of the deed of gift by which the materials were acquired. The items might be so fragile that use has been limited except under certain special conditions. Advance notification might be required so that the collection can be retrieved from a remote storage location. This note details the nature of such restrictions, portions of the collection to which they might apply, classes of individuals authorized to use the materials, conditions under which they may be used, and the authorization for such restrictions (see 1.7B11).

Terms Governing Use and Reproduction Note

Here one finds information similar to that found in the previous note but from another perspective — restrictions on uses to which the materials may be put once access has been granted. These can be general like copyright restrictions, or they can be related to institutional policies, such as the reproduction of fragile materials (see 1.7B12).

Cumulative Index/Finding Aids Note

Descriptive catalog records are often supplemented by other, more detailed finding aids in the repository to assist the patron in identifying desired collections and locating useful material within them. These include registers, inventories, indexes, calendars, box lists, microfilm reel lists, etc., which will be described in more detail in the following section. This note announces the existence of such finding aids, their type, and availability (see 1.7B13).

Physical Description

The development of an absolutely uniform and consistent standard for the physical description of archival materials has been limited by several factors. There is great variation in the size and composition of the materials being described in different records. They include a variety of physical media and packaging. The information given may focus either on the extent of the materials, their number and volume, or on their packaging, how many boxes, etc., or on both. It may serve as descriptive or as collection and space management data, or as both. The choices made by different repositories represent local preferences for counting collection size and for conveying physical extent to the patron. Catalogers expecting greater uniformity of practice among repositories might be surprised at the range of possibilities encountered.

For single pieces, extent is expressed in familiar terms, as a volume or item, often supplemented by page, leaf or items counts. For example, "1 v. (ca. 200 items)" (see 1.5B2).

The statement of extent for collections may be expressed in several ways. It may be given as item counts (actual or estimated), extent (in cubic or linear feet/meters), or packaging matter (boxes, volumes) or various combinations of the above. More than one statement of extent might be required, particularly when there are multiple physical media, e.g., text and computer files. APPM retrospectively introduces into its descriptive conventions the concept, "material specified," which is derived from the MARC-AMC format.[14] Portions of a collection may be described separately, each introduced by an appropriate descriptive word or phrase. The sum of the individual statements should equal the total size of the collection.

- Diaries: 3 volumes
- Correspondence: 12 cubic ft. (see 1.5B)

As always, microforms complicate description. When a collection contains both text and microforms, separate statements of extent are given for each. This applies when an institution holds both original and microform copies of the same material and is describing both in the same record. It is also appropriate when some portions of a collection exist in the textual original and others only as microfilm copy. These are not uncommon situations. When the institution holds only a copy, the originals being elsewhere or no longer extant, the extent of the reproduction is given. Information about the collation of the originals is given in the Scope and Content Note (see 1.5B3).

Other elements of the physical description are more familiar. The dimensions of individual pieces, volumes, or packing containers may be given along with details about bindings, illustrations, etc. Dimensions of microforms, particularly for non-standard sizes are also noted (see 1.5C, 1.5D).

Archival Finding Aids

While catalog records as described above have a long history in archival practice, they have been by no means the universal, exclusive, or even primary access tool in archives as they have been in libraries. Over the years, a variety of instruments have been used to bring the user to the holdings. Calendars, brief item by item descriptions of correspondence organized chronologically, were once regularly prepared for manuscript collections. Some institutions have found it useful on occasion to create item or file level indexes. In the past, many government record series came into the archives with indexes prepared in the office of origin as a management tool. These all have fallen from favor due to the high costs of preparation.

Repository guides too have been popular in the past though they provide access at a very different level of detail. A typical guide contains brief collection or series level descriptions for all the holdings in an institution. Entries resemble an abbreviated version of a catalog description. Often formal publications, such guides have proven increasingly costly and difficult to produce on a timely basis. Online systems and national databases seem on one hand to obviate the need for such printed materials. On the other hand, the ability to download electronic records from such systems presents an opportunity for the archivist to produce guides on a regular or on-demand basis. These may appear as specialized bibliographies or comprehensive listings.

Currently, the most commonly employed finding aid is the inventory, which provides a general overview of a collection or series. It stands as a fortuitous compromise between the desire to provide detailed information and the practical limitations of collection size and staff resources. While not formally defined as to presentation, structure or content, inventories produced by a wide range of repositories exhibit very similar purposes and content. These include a biographical sketch/agency history, a discussion of collection scope and content, descriptions of the component series, and a container list. The latter may be general or a detailed listing of the titles of each box and folder. The relationship of the structure of the inventory to catalog records is obvious, though the former is often much more detailed. It is easy to see how the catalog record might be seen as a pointer to or an abstract of the inventory. Remember that the inventory prepared by the cataloger is the most complete surrogate for the collection and serves as the chief source of information for the catalog description.

These conventions do not comprise a static code. Archivists continue to work to define the elements and tools of description that meet users' needs within the restraints of institutional resources and available technologies. The archival community has shown increased commitment in recent years to working with other information professions in the development of common protocols. In describing the relationship between archival and library practice, Schellenberg observed that "The development of methodology is, obviously, a never-ending job. . . . New methods of control are being developed, using new devices that are the product of modern technology, for the methodology of a profession must be constantly revised and refined to meet its current problems."[15]

NOTES

1. Steven L. Hensen, *Archives, Personal Papers, and Manuscripts: a Cataloging Manual for Archival Repositories, Historical Societies, and Manuscript Libraries* (Washington: Library of Congress, 1983), 3.

2. For a complete glossary of archival terminology, see Frank B. Evans and others, "A Basic Glossary for Archivists, Manuscript Curators, and Records Managers." *American Archivist* 37(1974):415-433.

3. A more detailed presentation of archival theories and practice for arrangement and description may be found in David B. Gracy, *Archives & Manuscripts: Arrangement & Description* (Chicago: Society of American Archivists, 1973) and in Frederic Miller, *Arranging and Describing Archives and Manuscripts* (working title) to be published by the Society of American Archivists in 1990.

4. *Anglo-American Cataloguing Rules*, 2nd ed, 1988 revision (Chicago: American Library Association, 1988), 122-138.

5. For a history of the development of this work, see Steven L. Hensen, "Squaring the Circle: the Reformation of Archival Description in AACR2." *Library Trends* 36(1988), 539-551.

6. Steven L. Hensen, *Archives, Personal Papers, and Manuscripts, a Cataloging Manual for Archival Repositories, Historical Societies, and Manuscript Libraries*, 2nd ed. (Chicago: Society of American Archivists, 1989).

7. These include *Cartographic Materials: A Manual of Interpretation for AACR 2* (Chicago: American Library Association, 1982); Sue A. Dodd, *Cataloging Machine-Readable Data Files* (Chicago: American Library Association, 1982); *Bibliographic Description of Rare Books* (Washington: Library of Congress, 1981); Elizabeth Betz, *Graphic Materials: Rules for Describing Original Items and Historical Collections* (Washington: Library of Congress, 1982); and Wendy White-Hensen, *Archival Moving Image Materials: A Cataloging Manual* (Washington: [1984]).

8. *Anglo-American Cataloguing Rules*, 1.

9. The author acknowledges the work of Nancy Sahli, first cataloger of the William Provenance Papers.

10. Hensen, *Archives, Personal Papers, and Manuscripts*, 2nd ed., 13.

11. Ibid., 28.

12. *Anglo-American Cataloguing Rules*, 257-273.

13. *Library of Congress Rule Interpretations*, 2nd ed. (Washington: Library of Congress, 1989), Chap. 11.

14. *USMARC Format for Bibliographic Data* (Washington: Library of Congress, 1988).

15. T.R. Schellenberg, *The Management of Archives* (New York: Columbia Press, 1965), 18-19.

Choice and Form of Access Points According to AACR 2

Edward Swanson

SUMMARY. Bibliographic records are retrieved through the use of access points, headings for persons and corporate bodies who are responsible for the creation of the work(s) represented by the bibliographic record, or who have another relationship with the work(s). Part II of the *Anglo-American Cataloguing Rules*, 2d ed. (*AACR 2*) gives instructions for determining which access points should be assigned to a given bibliographic record and the form that those access points should have. This article covers the basic rules in *AACR 2* that are needed for determining which access points to assign to an archival or manuscript work (whether a collection or an individual item) and for determining the form of access points for personal names, geographic names, and corporate body names.

Once the bibliographic description of an item (which can be a collection or a single manuscript) has been prepared, the cataloger assigns relevant personal and corporate name headings in order to permit access to the item through a catalog, whether printed or online. These headings generally are referred to as access points, because they provide access to the item. Access points usually include a main entry (i.e., the person or body chiefly responsible for the creation of the item), added entries (i.e., other persons or bodies with secondary responsibility for the creation of the item or related to it in other than a subject relationship), and subject entries (i.e., persons or bodies about which the item contains information). In some cases titles also will be assigned as access points.

Part II of *AACR 2* deals with the choice of access points and the

---

Edward Swanson is Principal Cataloger, Minnesota Historical Society, Saint Paul, MN 55101.

35

form that those access points will take. Chapter 21 (2)[1] gives instructions for determining which heading, if any, is to be assigned as the main entry, and which other headings are to be assigned as added entries. Chapter 22 (3) deals with determining the form of heading used for personal names, chapter 23 (4) with the form of heading used for geographic names, and chapter 24 (5) with the form of heading used for names of corporate bodies. In addition, chapter 25 (6) treats establishing uniform titles, and chapter 26 gives instructions for making references from variant forms of a heading and between related headings. Four appendices include rules for capitalization, abbreviations, and numerals, and a glossary.

This article will deal with the rules in chapters 21, 22, 23, and 24. Subject headings are not treated, except insofar as a personal or corporate name heading used as a subject heading has the same form it would have if used as a main or added entry.

CHOICE OF ACCESS POINTS

The long standing practice in cataloging has been to select one heading as the "main" entry, the person or corporate body chiefly responsible for the creation of the work being cataloged. (Whether the main entry should retain its pre-eminence in this era of online catalogs with sophisticated searching techniques is outside the scope of this article.) It is assumed that one heading will continue to be selected as the main entry, and guidance will be given in determining which heading it should be.

Chapter 21 (2) begins with a general rule, 21.1 (2.1), which defines "works of personal authorship" and "entry under corporate body." There then follow a series of rules for determining the main entry in cases in which (a) one person or body is responsible for the work; (b) the work is by an unknown person or an unnamed group; (c) the work is by two or more persons or bodies; (d) the work is a collection or is produced under editorial direction; (e) the work is one for which different persons or bodies are responsible for different parts; (f) the work is a modification of another work; (g) there is mixed responsibility in a new work (e.g., an interview or a spirit communication); and (h) the work is related to another work. Rules

21.31-21.39 contain instructions for entering certain legal publications (such as laws and treaties) and certain religious publications (such as sacred scriptures).

In cataloging archival and manuscript collections, the rules for determining the main entry can be condensed into the following general guidelines (*APPM* 2.1). In those cases not covered here, reference should be made to the relevant rules in *AACR 2*.

Generally, the following types of personal papers will be entered under the heading for a person (*APPM* 2.1A):

1. the personal papers of an individual;
2. the personal papers of two or more individuals, where one of the persons can be considered more prominent, or one person's papers predominate;
3. family papers formed around or generated by members of one family;
4. artificial collections assembled by an individual (in which case the term "collector" is added to the heading);
5. an individual manuscript, letter, diary, etc.; and,
6. an oral history interview, either on audio or video tape or in transcription (in which case the term "interviewee" is added to the heading).

Generally, the following types of records will be entered under the heading for a corporate body (*APPM* 2.1B):

1. the corporate records of a single corporate body; and,
2. individual official or government documents.

In the case of a corporate body whose name has changed over a period of time, the main entry is made under the heading for the latest name represented in the records, and added entries are made under the headings for earlier names. If the records were in the custody of an agency other than the one responsible for creating them, the main entry is under the heading for the agency responsible for creating the records.

Generally, the following types of records will be entered under title (*APPM* 2.1C):

1. artificial collections that are known by a particular name;
2. personal papers of two or more individuals where no one person is more prominent or the papers of one individual do not predominate;
3. nonarchival corporate collections;
4. papers of multiple families; and,
5. manuscripts and collections of manuscripts of unknown origin or authorship.

Rules 21.29-21.30 (2.2-2.3) give instructions on additional (''added'') entries that are to be made for persons, corporate bodies, and titles that are related to the item being cataloged.

HEADINGS FOR PERSONS

Throughout the rest of this article two concepts must be kept in mind. The word ''name'' as used herein refers to the way a person or corporate body refers to itself or the way in which it most commonly is identified. The word ''heading'' refers to the way in which the cataloger structures that name to arrive at a uniform means of identifying the person or corporate body in the catalog entry. It doesn't matter if the heading is being used as a main entry, as an added entry, or as a subject entry; the same form of heading will be used in all cases.

It also must be kept in mind that this heading is not a biographical sketch of a person nor is it an organization chart of a corporate body. *AACR 2* has been criticized for not using full names of persons or complete hierarchies of corporate bodies in headings. It is not the purpose of a heading to take the place of other reference sources that can give much more detailed information than there is room for in a heading. What is aimed at is establishing a heading that will uniquely identify the person or corporate body, based on the form of name of that person or corporate body in most common usage.

The general rule for determining the name used for establishing the heading for a person is 22.1 (3.1), which states that one is to choose the name by which a person commonly is known. Among possible names that might be used are the person's real name, a pseudonym, a title of nobility, a nickname, initials, or another appellation.

The first priority for a source for determining the name by which a person commonly is known is given to the name used by the person in published works. The reason for this is simple: because published works can be widely distributed, it is this name that is likely to be the one by which most people know the person. Evidence for this usage in published works can be taken from the works themselves or from statements of responsibility in bibliographic records.

If the person has not published any works, the next choice for determining the name is the manuscript collection itself. During the preparation of the finding aid, the cataloger should record the various names used by the person and decide which of these is the predominant form. It must be kept in mind that one must be honest about this; one cannot start with a form that the cataloger prefers and then skew the information from the collection to give preference to that form.

If a predominant form cannot be determined from the collection, one uses the form found in references sources issued in the person's language or in the country of the person's activities. As a final choice, if none of the previous sources identify a predominant form, one selects the latest form of name used by the person.

Rule 22.2B (3.2B) contains special instructions for selecting the name in the case of persons who have used one or more pseudonyms. If the person commonly is identified by a single pseudonym, the pseudonym is chosen as the basis for the heading.

• George Orwell
    (*not* Eric Arthur Blair)

If the person has used more than one pseudonym, or the real name and one or more pseudonyms, and has established separate bibliographic identities (i.e., the person uses one of the names for certain types of works, and another of the names for other types of works), rule 22.2B2 (3.2B2) instructs that each name is to be used to establish the heading for the particular type of works identified by that name. These multiple headings are connected by see-also references.

- Charles L. Dodgson
  (real name used in his theological and mathematical works)

- Lewis Carroll
  (pseudonym used in his literary works)

Rule 22.2B2 can be applied to a person who uses one or more pseudonyms for published works (and for whom, therefore, the headings have been established under the pseudonyms) but who uses his or her real name for personal papers. In other words, the name used in creating personal papers can be considered to constitute a separate bibliographic identity.

If a person is a contemporary author who uses multiple pseudonyms or the real name and one or more pseudonyms, rule 22.2B3 instructs that a heading is to be established for each name and used for the works in which that name appears. These multiple headings also are connected by see-also references. The LCRI for 22.2B defines "contemporary" as living authors, as well as any author who lived in the 20th century and whose literary activity primarily is within this century.

- Agatha Christie
  (first married name used in some works)

- Agatha Christie Mallowan
  (second married name used in some works)

- Mary Westmacott
  (pseudonym used in some works)

In the case of a person using multiple names who neither is contemporary nor has established separate bibliographic identities, rule 22.2B4 instructs that one name is selected on the basis of the name by which the person has come to be identified in later editions of his or her works, in critical works, or in other references sources, in that order of preference. See references are made from the other names.

If multiple headings are established for a person on the basis of rule 22.2B2 or 22.2B3, a "basic heading" is selected according to the instructions in LCRI 22.2B. The authority record for this "basic heading" is used to link all headings and also is used as the subject heading in the case of works that deal with some or all of the names used by the person. (If a work deals with the person's activities under only one name, however, the heading for that name would be used as the subject heading for that work.)

In the case where a person has changed name, rule 22.2C (3.2C) instructs that one is to use the later name as the basis for the heading unless the earlier name is likely to remain the one by which the person is better known.

- Grace Fields
  (*not* Grace Stansfield)
  (*stage name by which she commonly is known*)

but

- Edna St. Vincent Millay
  (*not* Edna St. Vincent Millay Boissevain)

Probably more common than the necessity to choose among different names is the necessity to choose among different forms of the same name. Rule 22.3A (3.3A) deals with cases where the forms of a name vary in fullness. In this case, the first choice is to use the form most commonly found. If that can't be determined, the next choice is the latest form. If there is doubt as to which is the latest form, one chooses the fuller or fullest form.

- Edw. T. Peterson
  (*most common form*; *occasional forms*: E. T. Peterson; Edward T. Peterson)

- Rachel Trickett
  (*most common forms*; *occasional forms*: M. R. Trickett; Mabel Rachel Trickett)

- Paul Cheney
  (*most common form*; *occasional form*: Paul B. Cheney)

- L. P.Colman
  (*usage*: Laurence Colman; L. P. Colman; *L. P. Colman is a fuller form*)

See references are made from the forms not chosen.

Once the name by which the person is identified has been chosen, one goes to rules 22.5-22.11 (3.5-3.9) to determine the heading. Rule 22.5 (3.5) deals with names that include a surname, and includes special rules for names in which an element other than the first is treated as a surname, for compound surnames, for surnames with separately written prefixes, and for prefixes hyphenated or combined with surnames.

For names not including a surname, rule 22.6 (3.6) includes instructions for entering names under a title of nobility, 22.8 (3.7) for entering names under a given name, 22.10 (3.8) for entering names under initials, letters, or numerals, and 22.11 (3.9) for entering names under a phrase.

Additions to Headings

Rules 22.12-22.16 (3.10-3.13) are instructions for additions to names in establishing the heading. Rule 22.12 (3.10) deals with additions to names of noblemen and noblewomen who are not entered under the title of nobility, as well as the addition of British terms of honor (e.g., Sir, Dame). Additions to names of saints are treated in rule 22.13 (3.11), and to headings for spirit communications in rule 22.14.

Instructions are given in rule 22.15 (3.12) for additions to names entered under surnames. Generally this is applicable in cases where the person is identified only by the surname without forename(s).

- Moses, Grandma

In cases where a woman is identified only by her husband's name, the term of address is included in the heading. The LCRI for rule 22.15 instructs that this term of address is to be added *following* the forename(s) in order to achieve proper filing sequence.

- Campbell, Patrick, Mrs.

Rule 22.16 (3.13) includes instructions for additions to names entered under given name, etc. These include rules for royalty, for consorts of royal persons, and for children and grandchildren of royal persons (22.16A (3.13A)).

- Karl XIV Gustaf, King of Sweden
- Louise, Queen, consort of Gustaf VI Adolf, King of Sweden
- Désirée, Princess, granddaughter of Gustaf VI Adolf, King of Sweden

Rules also are given for additions to names of popes, of bishops, etc., and of other persons of religious vocation entered under given name.

- John Paul I, Pope
- Mary Margaret of the Holy Martyrs, Sister
- Damien, Dom

Rules 22.17-22.19 (3.14-3.16) deal with additions to distinguish identical names. These include dates (22.17 (3.14)), fuller forms (22.18 (3.15)), and distinguishing terms (22.19 (3.16)). If two or more persons have identical headings, dates (if known) are added to them to distinguish one person from the other.

- Smith, John, 1924-
- Smith, John, 1941-

Rule 22.17 (3.14) includes a listing of various types of dates that might be added, e.g., birth date, death date, birth and death dates, etc. The rule also includes an option for adding these dates even if there is not a need to distinguish one person's heading from another's. The LCRI instructs that the option is to be applied if the date(s) are known at the time the heading is established. It also is Library of Congress practice that once a heading has been established with only a birth date or only a death date, it generally is not changed only if the other date becomes known.

- Kirkwood, James, 1930-
  (*not changed to* Kirkwood, James, 1930-1989)

If dates are not available to distinguish identical headings, rule 22.18 (3.15) instructs one to add a fuller form of name if known. This might include the full form of name(s) represented in the heading by initials or abbreviations or unused forenames. These additions are made in parentheses following the forename(s) and preceding the date(s).

- Lindbergh, Charles A. (Charles August)
- Lindbergh, Charles A. (Charles Augustus)

In some cases it might include unused names or initials that are not represented in the heading.

- Clark, Elizabeth (Ann Elizabeth)
- Clark, Elizabeth (Elizabeth Griggs)
- Clark, Elizabeth (Elizabeth L.)

This rule also contains an optional provision for applying the rule when there is not a need to distinguish among identical headings. However, in this case one is limited to adding a fuller form only if that part of the heading already is represented in the heading by an initial or abbreviation. If the heading consists of a surname and a term of address, the unused forenames may be added. The LCRI instructs that these additions are to be made if the information is known at the time the heading is established.

- Neill, Edward D. (Edward Duffield)
- Taylor, E. G. R. (Eva G. R.)
- Cox, Wm. T. (William Thomas)
- M. Alicia (Mary Alicia), Sister
- Moses, Grandma (Mary Robertson)

but

- Welch, Denton
    (*not* Welch, Denton (Maurice Denton))

In cases where neither dates nor fuller forms are available to distinguish identical headings, rule 22.19 (3.16) instructs adding distinguishing terms to one or all of the headings to differentiate among them. Generally these are such things as terms of address, titles of position or office, initials of academic degrees, etc., that appear with the person's names in works by the person or in reference sources. If the name is entered under given name, etc., the addition is made in parentheses; if the name is entered under surname, the addition is made following the forename(s) and preceded by a comma.

- Thomas (Anglo-Norman poet)
- Thomas (Notary)
- Dyer, Will
- Dyer, Will, wool merchant

Finally, if there is no way to distinguish among two or more otherwise identical names, rule 22.20 (3.17) instructs that the same heading is to be used for all.

GEOGRAPHIC NAMES

Chapter 23 (4) deals with establishing names of geographic entities. These names commonly are used as additions to corporate names (see rules 24.4C (5.4C) and 24.7 (5.7B4)), as names of governments, and as subject headings for the geographic areas.

Rule 23.2A (4.2A) instructs one to use the English form of the name of a place if there is one in general use. In the case of geographic names, one goes immediately to reference sources, generally gazetteers, to determine this. For place names in the United States, the preferred source is the Rand McNally *Commercial Atlas & Marketing Guide;*[2] for Canadian place names, *Canadiana Authorities;*[3] and for other countries, the series of gazetteers published by the United States Board on Geographic Names.

If there is no English form, use the form in the official language of the country. If the country has more than one official language, use the form found most commonly in English-language reference sources.

As with corporate bodies, if the name of a place changes, establish a new heading under the new name and link it with the former name with see-also references.

The rules in 23.4 (4.4) deal with additions to place names. If the place name is being used as an entry element, an addition to it is made in parentheses.

• Chicago (Ill.)

On the other hand, if the place name itself is being used as an addition to another name, the entire place name is enclosed in parentheses, and the name of the larger place is separated from the name of the smaller place by a comma.

• Water Tower Place (Chicago, Ill.)

Specific additions made to place names are covered in rules 23.4C-23.4F (4.4C-4.4F). For places in Australia, Canada, Malaysia, the United States, the U.S.S.R., and Yugoslavia, no addition is made to the name of a state, province, territory, etc. (23.4C (4.4C)). For places located within a state, province, territory, etc., of one of these six countries, the name of the state, etc., is added to the name of the place. Abbreviations that may be used as additions to place names are given in Appendix B.14.

• California (*not* California (U.S.))
• San Jose (Calif.)

For places in the British Isles, no addition is made to the headings for England, the Republic of Ireland, Northern Ireland, Scotland, Wales, the Isle of Man, or the Channel Islands (23.4D (4.4D)). For places located within one of those parts of the British Isles, the additions to be used are "England," "Ireland," "Northern Ireland," "Scotland," "Isle of Man," and "Channel Islands."

• England (*not* England (U.K.))
• Oxford (England)

For all other places, the addition to be used is the name of the country (23.4E (4.4E)).

• Göteborg (Sweden)

Rule 23.4F (4.4F) gives instructions for further additions that are to be made to geographic names when it is necessary to distinguish between two or more places with the same name. Generally one includes the name of an intermediate place; for places in the United States, this generally is the name of the county.

- Washington (Le Sueur County, Minn.)
- Washington (Olmsted County, Minn.)

When it is considered necessary to identify the place, for example when establishing the heading for a named part of a city, the name of the smaller place is included in the addition.

- Bronx (New York, N.Y.)

HEADINGS FOR CORPORATE BODIES

Unlike the other chapters in *AACR 2*, chapter 24 basically is not a chapter of rules. One could say (only semi-facetiously) that chapter 24 comprises one rule and forty pages of exceptions.

The criteria for identifying a corporate body are given in rule 21.1B1. It must be a group that acts or can act as an entity *and* it must have a name. The rule gives further guidance on how to determine if the body has a name. Some examples of unnamed groups include:

- a committee of the Minnesota Association of Teachers of Scandinavian
- the commissioners appointed under the provisions of legislative act of February 4, 1873
- the citizens of Boston

Rule 24.1 (5.1) gives the general rule, which is to enter a corporate body directly under the name by which it commonly is identified, unless a later rule provides for entering it subordinately. The rule also gives guidance on how to treat names that contain or consist of initials and how to deal with romanization of names in nonroman scripts.

Unlike persons, who generally are entered under the latest name when the name has changed, a heading is established for each name a corporate body has had. That heading is used for works by or about the body when it had that name. See-also references are made to link these earlier and later name headings (see chapter 26 of *AACR 2* for guidance on making cross references).

Rules 24.2-24.3 (5.2-5.3) give guidance in how to select the name to be used for the heading when variant forms of the name appear. In establishing the heading for a government, generally one uses the name of the geographic area (as established on the basis of the rules in chapter 23 (4)) over which the government exercises jurisdiction (24.5E (5.5E)).

Additions to and Omissions from Corporate Headings

Instructions on additions to be made to names of corporate bodies are given in rule 24.4 (5.4). If the name of the body does not convey the idea of a corporate body, rule 24.4B (5.4B) instructs that a general designation be added to the name in parentheses. Note that the instructions are explicit: the addition must be a general designation and in English. In addition, it must be nonjudgmental. For example, "Terrorist group" would not be an appropriate designation to use. A more specific designation can be used in those cases when two or more bodies with the same name would also take the same general designation. Some examples of qualifiers include "Firm," "Musical group," "Church," "Ship," and the like.

- US West Direct (Firm)
- House of Hope (Church)

The rules in 24.4C (5.4C) give instructions on other additions to be made to the heading for a corporate body. The rule addresses first those cases where two or more bodies have the same or similar names. Additions are made to these names to distinguish one from the other (rules 24.4C2-24.4C9 (5.4C2-5.4C9) give instructions for particular types of additions).

- Carleton College (Kingston, Ont.)
- Carleton College (Northfield, Minn.)

The second part of the rule refers to cases where the addition aids in understanding the "nature or purpose of the body." This rule is vague on purpose. It is left up to the cataloger to decide if making the addition will aid the user in understanding the nature or purpose of the body. LCRI 24.4C directs that in cases of doubt one should not make the addition. When dealing with local materials, a strong case can be made for making the addition in most instances. Neither way is more correct. If a general designation was added to the name, and another addition is being made on the basis of these rules, the additions are separated by a space-colon-space.

- 75th Anniversary Committee (Milwaukee, Wis.)
- Poe Memorial Association (University of Virginia)
- House of Hope (Church : Saint Paul, Minn.)

Certain types of words are omitted from a name in creating the heading. First, an initial article is omitted unless the intent is to file on the article (rule 24.5A (5.5A)). This generally happens with pseudo-articles that are part of a personal or geographic name (e.g., El Greco Society; Los Altos Public Library). Second, terms indicating incorporation are omitted unless they are an integral part of the name or are needed to make it clear that the name is a corporate body (rule 24.5C (5.5C)).

- Citadel
    (*not* The Citadel)

- Brother's Touch
    (*not* A Brother's Touch)

- Abingdon Freight Forwarding Agency
    (*not* Abingdon Freight Forwarding Agency Ltd.)

but

- Cobblestone Antiques, Inc.

Rule 24.7 gives special instructions on omissions from and additions to headings for conferences. It must be remembered that this is not a rule for establishing the heading for a conference, but only for making omissions from and additions to that heading once it has been established on the basis of the general rules. These instructions apply both to conferences entered under their own names and those entered subordinately under the heading for a higher or related body. Words to be omitted include those indicating number, frequency, and year of meeting. Additions include numbering of the conference, year of meeting, and venue. The additions are made in their own set of parentheses, and the elements are separated from each other by a space-colon-space. LCRI 24.7B gives guidance in deciding between using the name of a city or the name of an institution as the venue of a conference.

- Nutrition Conference
  (*not* Annual Nutrition Conference)

- American Library Association. Conference
  (*not* American Library Association. Annual Conference)

- National Eucharistic Conference (U.S.)
  (*not* Ninth National Eucharistic Conference)

- Bake-Off (Contest) (24th : 1973 : Beverly Hills, Calif.)

- Library Standards for Archival Description Workshop (1989 Aug. 14-15 : San Jose State University)

- Library Standards for Archival Description Workshop (1989 Oct. 23-24 : Saint Louis, Mo.)

- National Eucharistic Conference (U.S.) (9th : 1941 : Saint Paul, Minn., and Minneapolis, Minn.)

Subordinate Entry

Rules 24.12-24.27 deal with the entry of bodies that are subordinate or related to another body. Subordinate entry means that the heading for the body will be established as a subheading under the heading for the higher or related body. The process of establishing the heading is as follows:

1. Determine the heading for the higher body
2. Add the name of the subordinate body to the heading for the higher body; precede the name of the subordinate body with a period-space
3. If the name of the subordinate body includes the English word "Department," abbreviate it as "Dept."[4]
4. If the name of the subordinate body includes the name of the higher body, eliminate that name from the heading.

                    Name: Department of Education
      Heading for higher body: Minnesota
                     Add: Minnesota. {+} Department of Edu-
                            cation
               Abbreviate: Minnesota. Dept. of Education
                 Heading: Minnesota. Dept. of Education

                    Name: Carleton College Hockey Team
          Name of higher body: Carleton College
      Heading for higher body: Carleton College (Northfield, Minn.)
                     Add: Carleton College (Northfield, Minn.).
                            {+} ~~Carleton College~~ Hockey Team
                Eliminate: Carleton College (Northfield, Minn.).
                            {+} Carleton College Hockey Team
                 Heading: Carleton College (Northfield, Minn.).
                            Hockey Team

The same process is repeated if the name includes two or more
levels of hierarchy. In that case, the subheading for each level is
established, beginning with that for the highest level.

                    Name: Stated Meeting of the Synod of Lakes
                            and Prairies of the United Presbyterian
                            Church in the United States of Amer-
                            ica
  Heading for higher body: United Presbyterian Church in the
                            U.S.A.

Step 1:   *Add*: United Presbyterian Church in the
                            U.S.A. {+} Synod of Lakes and
                            Prairies of the United Presbyterian
                            Church in the United States of Amer-
                            ica
                Eliminate: United Presbyterian Church in the
                            U.S.A. {+} Synod of Lakes and
                            Prairies ~~of the United Presbyterian~~
                            ~~Church in the United States of Amer-~~
                            ~~ica~~
                 Heading: United Presbyterian Church in the
                            U.S.A. Synod of Lakes and Prairies

Step 2:   *Add*: United Presbyterian Church in the
                            U.S.A. Synod of Lakes and Prairies.
                            {+} Stated Meeting of the Synod of
                            Lakes and Prairies of the Presbyterian
                            Church in the United States of Amer-
                            ica
            Eliminate: United Presbyterian Church in the
                            U.S.A. Synod of Lakes and Prairies.
                            {+} Stated Meeting ~~of the Synod of~~
                            ~~Lakes and Prairies of the Presbyterian~~
                            ~~Church in the United States of Amer-~~
                            ~~ica~~
            Heading: United Presbyterian Church in the
                            U.S.A. Synod of Lakes and Prairies.
                            Stated Meeting

                    Name: Administrative
            Subordinate to: State Relief Agency *which is*
            Subordinate to: Minnesota
Heading for higher body: Minnesota

Step 1:   *Add*: Minnesota. {+} State Relief Agency
                    Heading: Minnesota. State Relief Agency

Step 2:   *Add*: Minnesota. State Relief Agency.
                            {+} Administrative
                    Heading: Minnesota. State Relief Agency. Ad-
                            ministrative

Rules 24.14 and 24.19 (5.14 and 5.19) might apply in some of
these cases where there are multiple levels of hierarchy, so that
some or all of the intervening levels of hierarchy will be omitted in
establishing the final form of the heading. This will be discussed in
more detail below.

The rules for determining whether a subordinate or related body
should be entered directly under its own name or as a subheading
under the heading for the higher body are found in rules 24.12-
24.27 (5.12-5.27). The rules are divided into three groups: (a)
bodies subordinate to nongovernment bodies or to government bodies entered directly under their own names (24.12-24.16 (5.12-
5.16)); (b) government bodies or entered under the heading for the

government (24.17-24.26 (5.17-5.26)); and (c) special rules for religious bodies and officials (24.27 (5.27)). In dealing with a subordinate body, one first examines its name in light of two general rules, 24.13 (5.13) for bodies subordinate to nongovernment bodies or to government bodies entered directly under their own names, or 24.18 (5.18) for government bodies that are entered under the heading for the government. Each of these two rules includes a list of types against which the name of the subordinate body is compared to determine if it will be entered subordinately or not. Although there are parallels between the two rules, there is a fundamental difference. All of the types in rule 24.13 (5.13) are based, like the general rule for nonsubordinate corporate bodies, on the body's name. However, this is true only of some of the types in rule 24.18 (5.18), and so it might be easier to consider that rule first.

Rule 24.18 (5.18) comprises eleven types of government bodies that are entered subordinately to the heading for the higher or related body. These types are best approached in two groups. First is the group of bodies that always will be entered subordinately based on the *nature of the body itself*, types 5-11. It doesn't matter what the body's name is; if the body is one of these types of bodies, it will be entered subordinately.

Type 5 is for agencies that are ministries or similar major executive agencies of national governments, ones that have no other agency above them.

• Great Britain. Ministry of Defence

Type 6 is for legislative bodies. Rule 24.21 (5.21) expands on type 6, giving instructions for the entry of legislative bodies, their chambers, committees, and other subordinate bodies.

• Australia. Parliament
    (*name*: Parliament of the Commonwealth of Australia)

Type 7 is for courts. Rule 24.23 (5.23) expands on type 7.

• United States. District Court (Virginia : Western District)
    (*name*: District Court for the Western District of Virginia)

Type 8 is for principal services of the armed forces. Rule 24.24 (5.24) expands on type 8.

- United States. Army. Minnesota Infantry Regiment, 13th
  (*name*: 13th Minnesota Infantry)

Type 9 is for a head of state or head of government. Rule 24.20 expands on type 9. It includes rules for those cases when the dates of incumbency and the person's name are added to the corporate heading for an individual head of state. Dates of incumbency and personal names are not added to corporate headings for individual heads of government. (For example, in the United States, the President is both the head of state and the head of government. In the United Kingdom, the Queen is the head of state; the Prime Minister is the head of government.)

- United States. President
  (*name*: President of the United States)

- United States. President (1945-1953 : Truman)

- Great Britain. Prime Minister
  (*but not*: Great Britain. Prime Minister (1979-   : Thatcher))

Type 10 is for embassies, consulates, etc. Rule 24.25 (5.25) expands on type 10.

- United States. Embassy (France)

Type 11 is for delegations to international or intergovernmental bodies. Rule 24.26 (5.26) expands on type 11.

- Uruguay. Delegación en las Naciones Unidas

Types 1 through 4, on the other hand, are entered subordinately or not based on the *nature or quality of the body's name*. In these types, one compares the *name* of the subordinate body with each of the types, and if the name meets the criteria of a type, it is entered subordinately. Unlike types 5-11, in types 1-4 it doesn't matter what the nature of the body is. Some names will fit more than one type, but as soon as it has been determined that the name fits one of the types, it is entered subordinately, and it is not necessary to compare it with the later types.

Type 1 is bodies whose names contain the words "Department," "Division," "Section," or "Branch," or their equivalents in another language. It doesn't matter how distinctive the name is. If the name contains one of these words, it is entered subordinately.

- Michigan. State Dept. of Education
  (*name*: Michigan State Department of Education)

Type 2 has two criteria that must be met before the body can be entered subordinately according to its provisions. First, the name must include a word "that normally implies administrative subordination." A list of such words in English, French, and Spanish as identified by the Library of Congress is included in Appendix A to this paper. Second, the name of the government must be required for the identification of the body. If the name of the subordinate body already includes the name of the government, or a reasonable surrogate of the name, it does not meet the second criterion, and the body's name does not fit as a type 2 heading

- Minnesota. State Relief Agency
  (*name*: State Relief Agency

but

- Georgia Board of Corrections
  (*not* Georgia. Board of Corrections)

- U.S. Fish and Wildlife Service
  (*not* United States. Fish and Wildlife Service)

Type 3 is bodies whose names are general in nature or do nothing more than indicate a geographic, chronological, numbered, or lettered subdivision.

- United States. National Park Service. Midwest Region
  (*name*: Midwest Region)

Type 4 includes those bodies whose names do not suggest that they are corporate bodies.

- Hennepin County (Minn.). Hennepin Parks
  (*name*: Hennepin Parks)

- Minnesota. State Relief Agency. Administrative
  (*name*: Administrative)

- Great Britain. HMSO Graphic Design
  (*name*: HMSO Graphic Design)

If, after having compared the name with each of the types in 24.18, it is determined that the name does not fit any of the types, one goes to rule 24.17 (5.17) and enters the body directly under its own name.

- Missouri Rehabilitation Hospital
  (*not*: Missouri. Rehabilitation Hospital)

- U.S. Fish and Wildlife Service
  (*not*: United States. Fish and Wildlife Service)

Rule 24.13 (5.13) deals with bodies that are subordinate either to a nongovernment body or to a government body that is entered under its own name. Generally rule 24.13 works in the same manner that rule 24.18 works for a government body that is entered under the name of the government. However, all types in rule 24.13 depend upon the *nature or quality of the name of the body*. There are no types in rule 24.13 where a body is entered subordinately based on the nature of the body itself.

Type 1 is similar to type 1 in 24.18. If the name includes the words "Department," "Division," "Section," or "Branch," or their equivalents in another language, the body is entered subordinately.

- Ashmolean Museum. Dept. of Western Art and Hope Collection of Engraved Portraits
  (*name*: Department of Western Art and Hope Collection of Engraved Portraits)

Type 2 is similar to type 2 in 24.18. The same two criteria apply: the name must include a word that "normally implies administrative subordination" and the name of the higher body must be required for identification. If the name of the higher body or a reasonable surrogate of it is present in the name of the subordinate body, the name does not fit under the provisions of type 2.

- Stanford University. Board of Athletic Control
  (*name*: Board of Athletic Control)
- British Library. Ad Hoc Working Party on Union Catalogues
  (*name*: Ad Hoc Working Party on Union Catalogues)

Type 3 is similar to type 3 in 24.18, bodies with names that are general in nature, or that do no more than indicate a geographic, chronological, numbered, or lettered subdivision.

- University of Wooster. Class of 1884
  (*name*: Class of 1884)
- U.S. Customs Service. Region IX
  (*name*: Region IX)

Type 4 includes those bodies whose names do not convey the idea that they are corporate bodies.

- Minnesota Historical Society. Continuing Education for Teachers
  (*name*: Continuing Education for Teachers)

Type 5 does not have an equivalent in rule 24.18. It deals with names of university faculties, schools, etc., that merely indicate a particular field of study. The LCRI to 24.13, type 5, expands its application also to names that merely indicate a field of activity or interest. As a general rule, if the name contains a proper name, it does not fit type 5.

- University of Texas at Austin. Humanities Research Center
  (*name*: Humanities Research Center)

but

- Bodleian Library
  (*not* University of Oxford. Bodleian Library)
- Curtis L. Carlson School of Management
  (*not* University of Minnesota. Curtis L. Carlson School of Management)

Type 6 also does not have an equivalent in rule 24.18. In this type, if the name of the body includes the entire name of the higher body, it is entered subordinately.

- Daughters of the American Revolution. Library
  (*name*: Daughters of the American Revolution Library)
- University of Colorado. Associated Alumni
  (*name*: Associated Alumni of the University of Colorado)

This means that some bodies that were eliminated as coming under the provisions of rule 24.13, type 2, still will be entered subordinately because the name does fit rule 24.13, type 6.

- OCLC. Users Council
  (*name*: OCLC Users Council)

The LCRI to 24.13, type 6, does exclude from its provisions those names that, if type 6 were applied, would result in a subheading that does not imply that it is a corporate body.

- Boys of the Manchester Grammar School
  (*not* Manchester Grammar School. Boys)

As in rule 24.18, if the name does not fit one of the types in rule 24.13, one goes to the general rule, in this case rule 24.12 (5.12), and enters the body directly under its own name.

- American Folklife Center
  (*not* Library of Congress. American Folklife Center)
- Rhodes House Library
  (*not* Bodleian Library. Rhodes House Library)

In some cases, a body will be subordinate to a body that in turn is subordinate to another body, or there might be several levels of hierarchy involved. Rules 24.14 and 24.19 (5.14 and 5.19) give instructions for cases when the intervening levels of hierarchy are to be omitted. Generally, the intervening levels are omitted unless the name of the subordinate body has been or is likely to be used by another body entered under the heading for the same higher body.

- Minnesota. Big Game Unit
  (*not* Minnesota. Section of Game and Fish. Big Game Unit)

- Minnesota. Section of Game and Fish
  (*not* Minnesota. Dept. of Conservation. Section of Game and Fish)

but

- Minnesota Historical Society. Library. Technical Services Dept.

- Minnesota Historical Society. Division of Archives and Manuscripts. Technical Services Dept.

This, then, is a brief introduction to the process of establishing headings for persons, places, or corporate bodies. Although some of the rules might appear arbitrary or capricious, they all are based on the single principle of enabling the cataloger to establish a heading that will uniquely identify the person or body based on the form of name most commonly used by that person or body.

NOTES

1. Throughout this article, references are to rule(s) in the *Anglo-American Cataloguing Rules*, 2d ed., 1988 revision (*AACR 2*) (Ottawa: Canadian Library Association; London: Library Association Publishing; Chicago: American Library Association, 1988). The related rule(s) in *Achives, Personal Papers, and Manuscripts*, 2d ed., by Steve Henson (*APPM*) (Chicago: Society of American Archivists. 1989), are given in parentheses following them. In addition, the reader should be aware of the *Library of Congress Rules Interpretations*, 2d ed. (LCRI) (Washington, D.C.: Cataloging Distribution Service, Library of Congress, 1989. (*With quarterly updates*) that explain, and in some cases expand upon, the rules in *AACR 2*.

2. Rand McNally and Company. *Commercial Atlas & Marketing Guide*. Chicago, Ill.: Rand McNally and Co. Annual.

3. National Library of Canada. *Canadiana Authorities*. Ottawa: National Library of Canada. Quarterly, with biweekly updates. Microfiche.

4. Although Appendix B does not include the word "Department" in the list of abbreviations, LCRI B.9 instructs to use the abbreviation in headings.

Appendix A

Words in English, French, and Spanish that "normally imply administrative subordination" for use with rules 24.13, type 2, and 24.18, type 2.

English	French	Spanish
administration	administration	administración
administrative (e.g., administrative office)	agence	agencia
	bureau	asesoría
	cabinet	comisaría
advisory ... (e.g., advisory panel)	comité	comisión
	commissariat	comité
agency	commission	coordinación
board	délégation	delegación
bureau	direction	diputación

committee	groupe de ...	dirección
commission	inspection	directoria
... group (e.g.,	mission	fiscalía
work group)	office	gabinete
office	secrétariat	gerencia
panel	service	grupo de ...
secretariat		jefatura
service		junta
task force		negociado
working party		oficina
		secretaría
but not		secretariado
council		servicio
program		superintendencia
project		

61

Subject Access to Archival
Materials Using LCSH

Richard P. Smiraglia

SUMMARY. This paper takes for granted that archival materials will be entered into a catalog in which *Library of Congress Subject Headings* (*LCSH*) will be used to provide access. The purposes of subject access are discussed. The matter of selecting the appropriate extent of subject cataloging for archival entities is raised. Archival entities will generally require more detailed subject cataloging than published materials. A scheme for subject analysis of archival materials is presented. *LCSH* is described briefly, and several archival entities are analyzed and provided with *LCSH* access points to illustrate the methodology employed. The chief advantages of using *LCSH* for archival materials are its availability, and its ability to cause archival materials to collocate topically with published materials in integrated online systems.

INTRODUCTION

There is continuing debate in the archival field over the efficacy of subject access for archival collections. Major issues include the concept of "aboutness" (how is it determined for archival materials?; is it of any use to information seekers?; should other concepts (occupation, form, genre) take precedence over topicality?); and the means of providing subject access (should LCSH be used, should it be adapted, or should archival thesauri be preferred?). These issues have been addressed by a broad spectrum of authors.[1]

This paper takes for granted that archival materials will be entered into a catalog in which *Library of Congress Subject Headings*

Richard P. Smiraglia is Senior Lecturer in the School of Library Service, Columbia University.

(*LCSH*)[2] will be used to provide access. Thus, the purposes of subject access are discussed briefly, then a scheme for subject analysis of archival materials is presented, *LCSH* is described, and several archival entities are analyzed and provided with *LCSH* access points to illustrate the methodology that can be used.

A fundamental aspect of the process of subject control of any material is that, like intellectual access (formulated in accord with *AACR2*), the process has two stages: first, *analysis* of the materials to determine the subject terms that must be used to describe the material; and second, *formulation of access points* to be embedded in the AMC bibliographic record.

Broadly, the purpose of subject control is:

1. To allow a user to find material of which the subject is known; and,
2. To allow a user to see what the repository has on a given subject.

Subject access points (subject headings) serve both purposes. First, they serve to identify the subject of particular archival collections, series, subseries, or items, and to facilitate direct topical retrieval of these collective entities. Second, and perhaps more important, subject headings allow a user to see the entire scope of a repository's holdings on a given topic by causing these bibliographic records to collocate, or appear side-by-side, under a subject heading in the catalog. Further, when *LCSH* is used to supply subject headings for AMC formatted records, the archival materials will collocate with published material on the same topic in an integrated bibliographic system (network or local), thus giving a user an opportunity to browse bibliographic records for both published works and primary source material under a topical heading. These functions are illustrated in Figure 1.

SUBJECT ANALYSIS

The process of subject analysis involves utilization of an appropriate scheme to assist the subject cataloger in determining precisely the subject content of the materials. Before undertaking analysis, a decision must be made about the depth of subject cataloging that will be utilized.[3] Subsequently, disciplines, topics, and forms are identified for each segment of a collection that will receive distinct subject cataloging. These are the topics of the section that follows.

Determination of Depth of Subject Cataloging

The first decision that must be made before subject cataloging can be undertaken is often seen as a management decision. That is, the extent (or depth) of subject cataloging must be determined. Subject cataloging can take place at any one of several levels. The most common approach in the subject cataloging of library materials is to use what is called the summary level. Summary level means that the analysis of the collection will proceed as though it were a single entity in its entirety. Thus, we reduce the subject content of a book to a single phrase that identifies its main topical theme and the specific forms in which that theme is treated.

For archival materials, treatment at the summary level would require a single phrase that *summarizes* the entire subject content of an archival collection and identifies the predominant forms that appear in the collection. Summary subject cataloging rarely will be appropriate for archival materials, however, because the depth of complexity of the materials will be lost in the gross generalizations that result from subject cataloging at the summary level, thus rendering the subject access points nearly meaningless.

The depth level, although rarely used in library cataloging, usually will provide a more meaningful approach to archival collections. To achieve subject cataloging at the depth level we break a collection of records into appropriate components and summarize each component individually.

A third option is to conduct subject cataloging at what is called the exhaustive level. At this level, the analysis of *every* component of a collection is undertaken, yielding the subsequent provision of headings for each and every component. Subject cataloging at the exhaustive level is very expensive and time-consuming and therefore will be utilized only in very special cases. Figure 2 illustrates

FIGURE 1: SUBJECT HEADINGS SERVE TWO PURPOSES

IDENTIFYING

FOUND IN RLIN AMC UNDER "CATTLE INDUSTRY#"*

Bayles, Grant L.

Interview, 7 Jul 1971.

54 pp. : typescript.

Summary: Recollections by Grant L. Bayles and Josephine Bayles of the cattle industry in San Juan County, Utah. Interview by Mary Risher.

1. Cattle industry and trade--Utah--San Juan County ....

COLLOCATING WITHIN A CATALOG

FOUND IN RLIN AMC UNDER "CATTLE INDUSTRY#"**

1) United States. Works Progress Administration. Writers Project.

"HISTORY OF GRAZING" FINAL DRAFT.   d-9554

UTSW88-A40   COLL MSS 8

2) Bayles, Grant L. INTERVIEW, 7 JUL 1971. d-9554   UTSX89-A3120   MSS

A 4008

FOUND IN RLIN AMC AND BOOKS UNDER "CATTLE INDUSTRY#"**

2 clusters in AMC

1) United States. Works Progress Administration. Writers Project.

"HISTORY OF GRAZING" FINAL DRAFT.   d-9554

UTSW88-A40   COLL MSS 8

2) Bayles, Grant L. INTERVIEW, 7 JUL 1971. d-9554   UTSX89-A3120   MSS

A 4008

FIGURE 1 (continued)

4 clusters in BRS

1) CAUSES AND POLICY IMPLICATIONS OF RECENT DECLINES IN IOWA'S

LIVESTOCK PRODUCTION AND MEAT PROCESSING INDUSTRIES / (Oakdale, Iowa

: Legislative Extended Assistance Group, 1985.)IAUL (c-9114 IaU-L)

IAUL (c-9114 IaU-L)

2) Halsell, H. H. (Harry H.). 1860-1957. MY AUTOBIOGRAPHY : (Dallas :

Printed for the author by Wilkinson Printing Company, c1948.)

CTYX (c-9114 CtY-BR)

3) Haley, J. Evetts (James Evetts). 1901- PASTORES DEL PALO DURO /

([Dallas? : s.n., 1934?])

CTYX (c-9114 CtY-BR)   NJPG (c-9114 NjP)

4) THE FEEDLOT / 2d ed. (Philadelphia : Lea & Febiger, 1977.)

DCLC (c-9110 DLC) .....

*LONg display

**MULtiple displays

summary- and depth-level subject cataloging for an archival collection.

Archival Management and the Depth Level

Perhaps an appropriate approach to determination of the extent (or depth) of subject cataloging for archival materials is to consider the amount of processing that is being conducted on a collection at the point that cataloging occurs. For example, a collection that is recently acquired, but not yet processed, might be represented in a catalog with a preliminary record, giving only the provenance and name of the collection, its chronological span, and brief annotations. At this point it would seem appropriate to summarize the subject content and apply appropriate subject headings to represent this summary description. The first example in Figure 2 illustrates this approach.

Subsequently, when processing is underway and the collection has been arranged into series and subseries, the depth level might be a better choice. For each component of the collection (that is, each series or record group, or each subdivision of a series or record group) a summary of the subject content can be made and appropriate headings applied to represent the subject content of each segment of the collection. In toto these headings will provide detailed subject access to the entire collection and summary access to each component of the collection. Also, by this time, finding aids might have been developed that will assist in the analysis of each segment of the collection. The second example in Figure 2 illustrates this approach.

The exhaustive level is probably appropriate only occasionally, when some segment of records is heavily used or considered to be of central importance to the repository or to some segment of the repository's users. Further, it is possible that exhaustive subject indexing can be provided not in the catalog, but rather in the finding aids. In this case, subject cataloging at the depth level can serve as a pointer in the catalog to a particular finding aid in which detailed content-indexing can be provided in either printed form or in computer-accessible databases.

Another approach to decision-making can rest on the question of

FIGURE 2: EXTENT (OR DEPTH) OF SUBJECT CATALOGING

SUMMARY LEVEL

Glass Blowers' Association of the United States and Canada.

Records, 1890-1940.

1 linear ft.

Chiefly administrative correspondence arranged chronologically within

volumes and indexed by records creator.

1. Glass Bottle Blowers' Association of the United States and

Canada--History--Sources. 2. Glass Bottle Blowers' Association of the

United States and Canada--Archives. 3. Glass blowing and working

industry--United States--Societies, etc.--History--Sources. 4. Glass

blowing and working industry--Canada--Societies, etc.--History--Sources.

5. Bottle industry--United States--Societies, etc.--History--Sources. 6.

Bottle industry--Canada--Societies, etc.--History--Sources. 7. Trade-

unions--Officials and employees--Correspondence.

DEPTH LEVEL

Glass Blowers' Association of the United States and Canada.

    Records, 1890-1940.

      1 linear ft.

Correspondence arranged chronologically within volumes, and indexed by records creator.

The Glass Bottle Blowers' Association of the United States and Canada (GBBA) was organized in 1868 as the Independent Druggist Ware Glass Blowers' League. It affiliated with the Knights of Labor in 1886 and withdrew from this affiliation in 1891 to become the United Green Glass Workers' Association of the United States and Canada, assuming its present name in 1895.

Chiefly administrative correspondence; also minutes, clippings, and a report on hearings on H.R. 16928.

The records include correspondence (1860-1915) (3 bound volumes of carbons and originals) containing letters from the Knights of Labor discussing possible amalgamation of the American Flint Glass Workers Union

FIGURE 2 (continued)

(AFGWU) and the GBBA; letters from Denis A. Hayes (president, GBBA) regarding jurisdiction, machinery, wage and price guidelines; letter (1897) discussing amalgamation of GBBA with Prescription Bottle Department of AFGWU; protest of "Danbury Hatters Case" (Sherman Antitrust, 1910); jurisdictional dispute with AFGWU (1909); manufacturers beginning production of bottles during 'summer shop" (1911); minutes and resolutions of committee to settle jurisdictional disputes between GBBA and AFGWU. Major correspondents include D.A. Hayes (president, GBBA), Frank Morrison, Samuel Gompers, J.W. Rowe (president, AFGWU), and C.E. Voitle (president, AFGWU). Additional materials include (1 bound volume) proceedings/minutes of conferences held between representatives of GBBA and AFGWU (1911); credential certificate for Harry Jenkins (1900); report of hearings on H.R. 16928 regarding regulation of storage of food products in District of Columbia, with statements by Harry Jenkins (1910); and souvenir booklet of GBBA "Golden Anniversary Convention" (1927) . . . .

1. Glass Bottle Blowers' Association of the United States and Canada--History--Sources. 2. Glass Bottle Blowers' Association of the United States and Canada--Archives. 3. Glass blowing and working industry--United States--Societies, etc.--History--Sources. 4. Glass blowing and working industry--Canada--Societies, etc.--History--Sources. 5. Bottle industry--United States--Societies, etc.--History--Sources. 6. Bottle industry--Canada--Societies, etc.--History--Sources. 7. Trade-unions--Officials and employees--Correspondence. 8. Hayes, Denis A.--Correspondence. 9. Gompers, Samuel, 1850-1924--Correspondence. 10. Morrison, Frank--Correspondence. 11. Rowe, J. W.--Correspondence. 12. Voitle, C. E.--Correspondence. 13. Knights of Labor. 14. American Flint Glass Workers' Union. 15. Collective labor agreements--Bottle industry--United States--History--Sources. 16. Collective labor agreements--Bottle industry--Canada--History--Sources. 17. Food--Packaging--Law and legislation--Washington (D.C.)--History--Sources.

significance of any particular archival collection. That is, the archivist can determine whether some set of records is being acquired for some definite purpose, in which case depth- or exhaustive-level cataloging will be appropriate. For records that have been acquired incidentally (e.g., a large collection of manuscript drafts is acquired from a prolific author, along with the author's collection of newspaper clippings), the summary level can be appropriate. In our fictitious example, the manuscript drafts have been acquired deliberately but the newspaper clippings were a surprise. All of the clippings come from major newspapers that are indexed by newspaper reference sources; thus any importance that might be attached to the clippings resides in the fact that they were compiled by this particular creator and that they accompanied his or her papers. They are not significant primary sources in and of themselves. Consequently a summary approach to cataloging the clippings would be appropriate (because access to them is available in more efficient ways), while a depth-level analysis might be applied to the papers themselves.

Stages and Methods of Subject Analysis

Following management decisions about the level or depth of subject cataloging to be attempted, the next stage is to analyze the collection and its various components to determine the appropriate subjects that will be represented by subject headings in the catalog. At this point it is useful to consider the fact that "subject" is a very broad term, which encompasses concepts such as the discipline in which a given topic is treated, the specific topic or topics that are represented, and the forms in which the material represents a given topic.

Figure 3 illustrates the categories that must be considered when analyzing archival materials to determine their subject content. Note that the concept "topic" is further subdivided into two major categories, provenance (which identifies the source of the materials and the activity that caused them to be gathered), and cultural terms (which identify any chronological and geographic orientation of any specifically topical material). Note further that there are three categories of form terms: (1) intellectual forms, such as historical

FIGURE 3: ANALYTICAL SCHEME*

Discipline

Topic

    Provenance

        Creator, Function, Activity

    Cultural orientation

        Chronological

        Geographic

Form

    Intellectual

    Physical

    Presentation

* From Smiraglia, Richard P., "From Soup to Nuts: A Methodology for Providing Subject Access to Archival and Manuscript Collections." Paper presented at the annual conference of the Society of American Archivists, October 25, 1989, St. Louis Mo.

sources; (2) physical forms, such as diaries or correspondence; and (3) presentation forms, such as statistics, or the language in which the materials were created.

This scheme provides the cataloger with general guidelines for analyzing the subject content of every segment to be cataloged. That is, once terms have been identified in all of the applicable categories, the product is a summary of the subject content for which subject headings will be selected next. Figure 4 shows both summary- and depth-level analysis for the collection in Figure 2.

In order to provide sufficient information for the user to be able to make an informed choice and to understand why any particular record has been retrieved in response to a system query, it is necessary for the description in the AMC record to provide all terms that will be used to generate subject headings. In extreme cases (such as very large complex collections) a hint might suffice.

In the summary analysis we apply the analytical scheme to identify in very broad terms the subject content of the entire collection. For depth analysis we break the collection into appropriate components: (1) the correspondence; (2) the conference minutes, clippings, and certificate; (3) the report on H.R. 16928; and (4) the booklet. We now are conducting a summary analysis of *all* of this correspondence. However, we disregard the specific topics mentioned in the scope note, which would be considered only if we were attempting exhaustive analysis. The conference minutes and certificate are disregarded, again because their broad content has been covered in prior stages of analysis. Specific analysis of the content of each would be conducted only at the exhaustive level. Similar summary analyses are conducted for both the hearing report and the anniversary booklet. Notice that for both the report and the booklet we have identified the topics treated within, rather than the items themselves. Analytical added entries could be made (using *AACR2*) to note the presence of these items in the collection. Content analysis of the booklet or the report could be conducted at the exhaustive level, if it were deemed appropriate.

The process of subject analysis involves two simple steps: (1) making a decision about the depth of subject cataloging to be undertaken; and (2) analyzing the collection in appropriate seg-

FIGURE 4: SUBJECT ANALYSIS

SUMMARY LEVEL

Glass Blowers' Association of the United States and Canada.

Records, 1890-1940.

1 linear ft.

Chiefly administrative correspondence arranged chronologically within

volumes and indexed by records creator.

Discipline: glass blowing industry

Topic

Provenance

Creator: GBBA

Function: trade association

Activity: administration

Cultural orientation

Chronological: 1890-1940

Geographic: United States and Canada

FIGURE 4 (continued)

Form

Intellectual: primary sources

Physical: correspondence

DEPTH LEVEL

Glass Blowers' Association of the United States and Canada.

Records, 1890-1940.

1 linear ft.

...

The records include correspondence (1860-1915) (3 bound volumes of
carbons and originals) containing letters from the Knights of Labor
discussing possible amalgamation of the American Flint Glass Workers Union
(AFGWU) and the GBBA; letters from Denis A. Hayes (president, GBBA)
regarding jurisdiction, machinery, wage and price guidelines; letter (1897)
discussing amalgamation of GBBA with Prescription Bottle Department of
AFGWU; protest of "Danbury Hatters Case" (Sherman Antitrust)(1910);
jurisdictional dispute with AFGWU (1909); manufacturers beginning
production of bottles during 'summer shop" (1911); minutes and resolutions

of committee to settle jurisdictional disputes between GBBA and AFGWU.
Major correspondents include D.A. Hayes (president, GBBA), Frank Morrison,
Samuel Gompers, J.W. Rowe (president, AFGWU), and C.E. Voitle (president,
AFGWU).

Analysis begins at the summary level, to which we add

1) The administrative correspondence:

    Topic: Collective labor agreements

    Form

    Physical: correspondence (including name of each correspondent)

Additional materials include (1 bound volume) proceedings/minutes of
conferences held between representatives of GBBA and AFGWU (1911);
credential certificate for Harry Jenkins (1900);

No analysis.

Report of hearings on H.R. 16928 regarding regulation of storage of
food products in District of Columbia, with statements by Harry Jenkins
(1910);

FIGURE 4 (continued)

We analyze this segment, including:

Topic: H.R. 16928

    Regulation of storage of food products

Geographical: Washington (D.C.)

Form:

    Physical: Hearing report

and souvenir booklet of GBBA "Golden Anniversary Convention" (1927)

. . . .

Topic: GBBA

Form: booklet

ments. We will return to this example to select LC subject headings after a brief introduction to the use of *LCSH*.

THE LIBRARY OF CONGRESS SUBJECT HEADINGS

The *Library of Congress Subject Headings* is probably the predominant list of subject terms used in bibliographic cataloging in North America. *LCSH* utilizes subject cataloging principles devised by Charles Cutter in 1876, principles that later were refined and modified by David Haykin in the mid-twentieth century, and that continue to be refined by the Library of Congress Subject Cataloging Division, often with the advice of the American Library Association Subject Analysis Committee. The terms in *LCSH* originally were derived from a combination of terms compiled by the American Library Association and the Harvard University Library, first produced as a printed list at the Library of Congress in 1909.[4]

The list is published in printed form annually and is now in its thirteenth edition. Additionally, the list appears in microfiche updated quarterly. It is also available in machine-readable form that is available either on tape or CD-ROM from the Library of Congress. The machine readable files are available online through OCLC and RLIN. In addition to the list, it is necessary to consult the *Subject Cataloging Manual (SCM)*,[5] in which detailed instructions on the formulation of geographic headings and the use of subdivisions can be found.

Guiding Principles

LCSH is built on a concept known as literary warrant. This means that the terms in the list are derived from the materials in the Library of Congress that are being cataloged. In other words, the presence of the terms in the list is warranted by their use in published literature and the need for LC catalogers to derive those terms for use as subject headings.

LCSH is a controlled vocabulary, and terminology is selected and used according to four principles. These are:

The User or Reader as Focus

Of course, LC's primary user-public is the Congress of the United States, but secondarily LC is a major research library. Thus terminology that will be useful for both Congressional and scholarly research is favored.

Unity or Uniformity

Headings should be uniform both within and across disciplines in order to maintain internal consistency of the list.

Specificity

At any point in subject cataloging, the most specific heading possible must be chosen to represent a concept. Thus, if material is about Siamese cats, we choose the heading SIAMESE CAT, not CATS, or FELIDAE.

Coextensivity

Headings assigned should be coextensive with the topic covered by the material, no more, no less. That is, if the material is about the anatomy of cats, the heading CATS—ANATOMY is chosen, because it precisely identifies the topic. In many instances (often because literary warrant means that some segments of the list are more highly developed than others), more than one heading must be used to achieve coextensivity. For instance, if material is about anatomy of Siamese cats, we must use two headings: SIAMESE CAT (which is an authorized heading in the list, but for which no subdivisions are available); and CATS—ANATOMY (which is the closest term possible that allows the subdivisioned —ANATOMY).

Syndetic Structure

Relationships between and among headings are indicated in the list in such a way as to display the hierarchies within which specific headings are located. That is, any heading in the list might be accompanied by a series of specific references. The types of references made are:

- BT = Broader term
- NT = Narrower term
- RT = Related term

Further, references also appear in the list to accomplish the control of vocabulary. That is, references are provided to assist both the cataloger and the user to move from terms that are not authorized for use to the appropriate authorized heading, and also from one authorized heading to another that might be of interest. These references take the form:

- UF = Used for
- SA = Search also under

Figure 5 illustrates this syndetic structure for the heading DIPLOMATICS. UF indicates that a reference from the term DOCUMENTS points to the heading DIPLOMATICS. BT indicates broader terms (those that precede DIPLOMATICS in a hierarchy) such as AUXILIARY SCIENCES OF HISTORY, CARTULARIES, etc. RT indicates related terms (those that arc on similar levels in other, related hierarchies) such as ARCHIVES, etc. And NT indicates narrower terms (those that follow DIPLOMATICS in a hierarchy) such as CHARTERS, COPYISTS, etc.

Figure 6 illustrates the heading AUTARCHY. In this example, in addition to UF and BT references, we are also given a SA instruction, which tells us that we might also wish to consider using the subdivisions — COMMERCIAL POLICY and — ECONOMIC POLICY under names of specific countries.

Types of Headings

Topical terms constitute the main headings found in bold type in printed versions of the list. Subdivisions are used to represent forms, geographical and chronological orientation, and in many instances to represent subcategories of a topic. Subdivisions are of three types: (1) specified, which are printed in the list and may only be used as specified; (2) free floating, which can be located in the *SCM* and used whenever appropriate; and (3) geographic, which are

FIGURE 5: SYNDETIC STRUCTURE

Diplomatics (May Subd Geog)*

[CD1-724]

UF Documents

BT Auxiliary sciences of history

Cartularies

Historiography

History

History--Sources

RT Archives

Manuscripts

Manuscripts--Facsimiles

Paleography

NT Charters

Copyists

Document writing, Chinese

Formularies (Diplomatics)

Seals (Numismatics)

Signatures (Writing)

Tironian notes

*LCSH, 13th ed., p. 1129.

FIGURE 6: SYNDETIC STRUCTURE, (SA)

Autarchy

[HD82–HD85]

Here are entered works on economic self-sufficiency.

UF Economic self-sufficiency

    Self-sufficiency, Economic

BT Commercial policy

    Economic policy

SA subdivisions Commercial policy and Economic policy under names of countries.

*LCSH, 13th ed., p. 294.

85

constructed according to instructions in the *SCM* and may be used whenever the indication *"(May subd geog)"* appears in the list.

- Specified: ELECTRIC MOTORS — LUBRICATION
- Free floating: ELECTRIC LAMP INDUSTRY — ABBREVI-ATIONS

    (the subdivision — ABBREVIATIONS is found in *SCM* H1095)
- Geographic: DAYLILIES — MINNESOTA — ST. PAUL

Geographic subdivision is always *indirect* except when otherwise specified in *SCM*. This means that subdivision always proceeds indirectly through the larger jurisdiction, when appropriate (as opposed to direct subdivision, which would proceed directly to the smaller jurisdiction). In the example above, the material being cataloged is about Daylilies in St. Paul, Minnesota. The city of St. Paul is located in the state of Minnesota, which is a larger jurisdiction. Thus, the subdivision is indirect, proceeding through — MINNESOTA to — ST. PAUL.

Additionally, many headings in the main list and many free floating subdivisions in the *SCM* are accompanied by scope notes, which indicate the appropriate usage of the headings or subdivisions. Library of Congress classification numbers also appear in brackets next to many headings, to indicate the disciplines from which the topical headings have been derived, and therefore the disciplinary context in which they may be used. Scope notes and classification numbers can be seen in Figure 6.

Finally, many names can be used as subject headings whenever the topic involved is a person, place, or corporate body that has a name. These headings are to be constructed according to *The Anglo-American Cataloguing Rules*, Second edition, as needed. They are not printed in the list unless specific references or subdivisions are required. Headings for geographic regions (for which there are no provisions in *AACR2*) are derived by LC subject catalogers and printed in the list.

Headings and Subdivisions Useful
for Archival Purposes

Because of the concept of literary warrant that governs the selection of headings for the list, few headings have been developed for specifically archival use. This, of course, is because the headings are generally derived from published literature and not from primary source materials. However, a few useful categories of headings that can receive archival applications exist. These are:

Correspondence

The *SCM* directs the use of a complex of headings for correspondence. This complex is explained at *SCM* H1480, and works like this:

* [name of the letter writer(s)] — Correspondence
* [name of the addressee(s)] — Correspondence
* [class of persons, or ethnic group] — Correspondence
* [special topics discussed in the letters]

Note that *SCM* H1480 specifies that these provisions may be used only for correspondence of individual persons.

History — Sources and Archives

SCM H1647 indicates that the subdivision — HISTORY — SOURCES may be used for historical source materials pertaining to a topic.

SCM H1230 indicates that the subdivision — ARCHIVES may be used under types of corporate bodies and educational institutions, classes of persons, ethnic groups, individual corporate bodies, educational institutions, persons and families, for collections of documentary material relating to these persons or institutions.

Manuscripts

Detailed instructions for formulating a complex of headings for manuscript collections and for individual manuscripts can be found at *SCM* H1855.

Genealogy and Local History

Detailed instructions for formulating a complex of headings for genealogical source materials, and for local historical materials can be found at *SCM* H1845.

Headings in the list that appear to be form terms often really are intended for use as topical headings for published works about the form. For example, the heading INTERVIEWS may be used only for works about the topic of interviews, not for examples of interviews. A very few may be used as form headings, but only when the scope notes so indicate; an example is ORAL HISTORY.

APPLICATION OF LCSH
TO ARCHIVAL BIBLIOGRAPHIC RECORDS

Now we can proceed to assign LC subject headings to our AMC record. The descriptive portion of the record must be completed first, to facilitate the process of subject analysis, and a decision about the extent (or depth) at which subject cataloging will be performed must be made. If in the course of subject analysis the cataloger decides that some concept not already represented in the scope note should be represented by subject headings, a phrase describing that concept should be added to the description at this point. The analysis phase is followed by the selection of headings.

The bibliographic records in Figure 2 indicate the LC subject headings that are appropriate for the analysis conducted previously. Note that in the summary example several headings have been chosen to achieve coextensivity. In particular, in order to indicate a geographical orientation, the heading BOTTLE INDUSTRY has been used twice, each time with one geographic subdivision. The subdivision — SOCIETIES, ETC. may be used under topical headings for materials that relate to societies. And the subdivision — HISTORY — SOURCES is the appropriate LC subdivision used to indicate that material is not directly topical, but rather is primary source material related to any topic, in this instance, the association.

In the depth example, headings have been added for each correspondent. The substantial amount of material treating jurisdictional disputes and labor agreements is represented by two headings for COLLECTIVE LABOR AGREEMENTS, each with the subdivision — BOTTLE INDUSTRY and geographic subdivision. The hearing report is represented by a heading for the topic of the hearings. And the booklet is represented broadly by a heading for the association with the subdivision — ANNIVERSARIES, which is free floating under the names of countries, cities, corporate bodies, historic and social movements, and historic events.

CONCLUSION

LCSH is a workable subject heading list for archival materials when used appropriately and in conjunction with careful subject analysis. There is no doubt that many other kinds of subject approaches to archival materials are available outside *LCSH* and these should be utilized to the fullest in addition to *LCSH* in AMC records. The chief advantages of using *LCSH* are that the list already is available, and that the resulting records will collocate in integrated systems with published materials on the same topics.

It is worth noting here that many of the problems archivists have encountered in their attempts to use *LCSH* for AMC records are the same problems that librarians not only have found, but repeatedly have complained about in recent years. It is possible that if the entire community of information professionals devoted to the control of recorded knowledge works together, better techniques for subject access will emerge in the not too distant future.

NOTES

1. See for example, Richard H. Lytle, "Intellectual Access to Archives: I. Provenance and Content Indexing Methods of Subject Retrieval." *American Archivist* 43 (1980): 64-75, and "Intellectual Access to Archives: II. Report of an Experiment Comparing Provenance and Content Indexing Methods of Subject Retrieval." *American Archivist* 43 (1980): 191-206; David Bearman, "Archives and Manuscript Control with Bibliographic Utilities: Challenges and Opportunities." *American Archivist* 52 (1989): 26-39; "Authority Control Issues and Prospects." *American Archivist* 52 (1989): 286-299; Mary Jo Pugh, "The Illusion of Omniscience: Subject Access and the Reference Archivist." *American Archivist* 45 (1982): 33-44; and Helena Zinkham, Patricia D. Cloud, and Hope Mayo,

"Providing Access by Form of Material, Genre, and Physical Characteristics: Benefits and Techniques." *American Archivist* 52 (1989): 300-319.

2. Library of Congress, Subject Cataloging Division, *Library of Congress Subject Headings*. 13th ed. (Washington, DC: Library of Congress, Cataloging Distribution Service, 1990).

3. I have borrowed and paraphrased the term "depth of subject cataloging" from the indexing field, where the term originated as "indexing depth."

4. See for example, Charles A. Cutter, *Rules for a Printed Dictionary Catalogue*. (Washington, D.C.: Government Printing Office, 1876); and David Judson Haykin, *Subject Headings: A Practical Guide*. (Washington, D.C.: Government Printing Office, 1951). Also, for brief history see Lois Mai Chan, *Library of Congress Subject Headings: Principles and Application*. 2nd ed. (Littleton, Colo.: Libraries Unlimited, 1986).

5. Library of Congress, Subject Cataloging Division. *Subject Cataloging Manual: Subject Headings*. 3rd ed. (Washington, DC: Library of Congress, Cataloging Distribution Service, 1988).

Authority Work for Transitional Catalogs

Marion Matters

SUMMARY. Archivists, like all other perpetrators of catalogs, are grappling with the role of authority control and the nature of authority work. The primary objective of authority work in transitional archival catalogs is to balance the headings management aspect of more traditional authority work with the historical/contextual aspect of enhanced authority work. Conformance with the standard requirements of headings management is necessary if archival materials are to collocate with other types of material in integrated catalogs. Techniques for archival headings management are described. Two additional objectives are to avoid duplication of work by sharing the results, and to foster the development of information systems that use the expensive authority work to support access.

To say that something is "in transition" often means that it is moving from a state that is clearly outmoded or dysfunctional toward some new state that is not clear at all. So it is with archival catalogs, just recently emerging from isolation into the larger bibliographic universe.[1] They might be in transition from manual to automated control, or from creaky old automated files (or merely "fast paper")[2] to—well, something more sophisticated. They might be in transition from small local files to segments in larger institutional or national databases. In exploring archival information sys-

Marion Matters is Senior Archival Collections Cataloger at the Minnesota Historical Society, 1500 Mississippi St., St. Paul, MN 55101. During 1988-1989, while on leave from the Minnesota Historical Society, she served as Automation Program Officer for the Society of American Archivists. In this position she coordinated workshops on the USMARC AMC format, *Anglo-American Cataloguing Rules*, and Library of Congress Subject Headings, helped produce the second edition of *Archives, Personal Papers, and Manuscripts*, Steven Hensen, compiler (Chicago: Society of American Archivists, 1989), and was a member of the Working Group on Standards for Archival Description.

tems in transition, archivists, like all other perpetrators of catalogs, are grappling with the role of authority control and the nature of authority work.[3]

Traditionally (that is, in library literature) authority work is equated with support for headings management: establishing a single unique form of name as the authorized heading, defining its scope if necessary, making references from nonauthorized forms, and recording documentation of the decisions made (e.g., sources consulted, results of research).[4] Authority work creates authority records (usually one for each authorized heading), which are assembled in authority files. The authorized headings, which are used as access points in bibliographic records, provide the links between the bibliographic records in a catalog and the authority records in an authority file.[5]

But archivists also have articulated a need for authority work that goes well beyond the establishment of authorized headings.[6] When archivists research and record information about the history or biography of records creators, about their activities and functions, or about the forms of material they create, the establishment of an authorized form of name is a byproduct. The information is primarily intended to promote understanding of — and access to — archival materials.[7] Such information also can be used to infer various relationships (topical, functional, chronological, geographical) within and between archival groups. Authority records that provide more than mere identification might be termed "enhanced," just as others have referred to enhanced bibliographic records, which provide more than simple bibliographic identification (e.g., tables of contents or indexes from the items cataloged).

In this expanded role, authority files would be reference files, linked with, but independent of, bibliographic files. Enhanced authority records might be similar to encyclopedia entries. Authority work would produce for enhanced authority records the biographical, historical, or other contextual scope notes that are typically now included in archival finding aids and "bibliographic" catalog records.[8]

Any authority work is wasted, however, when the links between authority files (enhanced or not) and bibliographic files (enhanced or not) are incomplete or nonexistent, as, for example, when the bibliographic file contains few or none of the references mandated by the authority file, or when the contextual data from an enhanced authority record is not easily available to users of the bibliographic file. In fact, we have few catalog systems that truly support linked authorities of any kind, much less linked enhanced authorities.

The primary objective of authority work in transitional archival catalogs, as I see it, is to balance the headings management aspect of more traditional authority work with the historical/contextual aspect of enhanced authority work — and in some cases to compensate for what ideal catalogs should do but transitional catalogs don't do. Two additional objectives should be to avoid duplication of work by sharing the results, and to foster the development of information systems that use the expensive authority work to support access.

In this discussion I will concentrate on just a few aspects of authority work for names of persons and corporate bodies and how they relate to the objectives of authority work for transitional archival catalogs. Subject authority work is beyond my scope here.

AUTHORITY WORK FOR HEADINGS MANAGEMENT

Conformance with the standard requirements of headings management is necessary if archival materials are to collocate with other types of material in integrated catalogs.[9]
That means:

1. Accepting and using headings that already have been established in standard authority files, like the Library of Congress Name Authority File (LCNAF).
2. Establishing new headings (even for local use) according to relevant standards, e.g., *Archives, Personal Papers and Manuscripts* (*APPM*) and *Anglo-American Cataloguing Rules* (*AACR 2*).[10]
3. Adding new headings to standard authority files whenever it is possible to do so; for LCNAF, through the National Coordinated Cataloging Program (NACO),[11] or indirectly through the *National Union Catalog of Manuscripts Collections* (*NUCMC*).[12]
4. Maintaining authority data, if not externally by contribution to

the LCNAF, then internally in local authority files, so that the work needed to establish a heading or reference need never be duplicated.[13]

5. Seeing that the references specified in authority records are used to facilitate access in public catalogs.

It seems simple enough. This is nothing new in authority control. But for the archivist new to this kind of authority work, obstacles seem to impede each step. The first three require adjustments either in attitude or procedure for archivists. The latter two are a problem for everyone (and for subject headings as well as name headings), and I will not cover them in any detail here.[14]

In order to use headings already established or to establish new headings according to relevant standards the archives must first invest in access to the source of established headings and to the rules for establishing new headings.[15] If the cost of such an investment seems unreasonable to the small archives, then the cost of learning to use the new tools will also be unreasonable; perhaps it cannot afford this kind of authority work at all. Unfortunately, the cost of not doing authority work is not well-documented, in libraries or archives.[16] The cost of doing authority work without reference to external standards (whether files or rules) is likewise undocumented. Logically, it would seem that learning and adopting existing standards should be less costly than creating new ones. But it might also be true that much of the high cost of authority work is the result of inefficiencies in searching multiple sources and in manual transcription of data from or about those sources into authority records, then into catalog records.

Still, it has been argued that shared authority work, especially the enhanced variety, offers for all cultural repositories exactly the kind of financial saving that libraries realized through shared cataloging.[17] Since shared authority work must be standard authority work, even at the local level it requires access to shared authority files, bibliographical databases, biographical and other reference works, gazetteers, etc.

Even if the outright cost is not prohibitive, the archives must still relinquish a certain amount of local control, and in some cases make significant changes from previous local practice.

WHO DOES WHO SAY THAT I AM?
AUTHORITY WORK FOR PERSONAL NAMES

Archivists are used to dealing with the "documentary remains"[18] of real people, not the literary output of "bibliographic identities." The transition from a focus on biography (enhanced authority work) to an equal focus on form of name, especially the predominant form of name (headings management authority work), is not difficult, but it might require an adjustment in procedure. In archival authority work we must often establish headings for people who functioned in the existential universe using rules that presume a bibliographic universe.[19]

Here is a sample sequence for the process of local name heading authority work (for either personal or corporate names).[20]

1. Start with the name as found in archival materials.
2. Check the public catalog (manual or online). If the name is found, record it, and proceed to step 3. If the name is not found, proceed to step 3.
3. Check LCNAF. If the name is found, assign the authorized heading and stop; except, if the form of heading found in LCNAF is different from a heading previously established (i.e., in older records in the public catalog), create mutual cross references for the public catalog (i.e., old forms are not changed). If the name is not found, proceed to step 4.
4. Establish the heading according to *AACR 2*, consulting published works, headings created previously, the materials being cataloged, and reference sources. In this process, check any available statewide or regional bibliographic database and the RLIN bibliographic database.
5. If the name is one of the following types (using Minnesota simply as an example), prepare LCNAF/NACO[21] entries: Minnesota state agencies; Minnesota cities or townships; Minnesota persons or organizations of statewide or broader significance; any name for which an earlier or later name heading appears in LCNAF; any heading used on three or more records in public catalogs; any heading that requires extra effort to establish; any heading that requires a cross reference that is not

obvious from the heading itself (e.g., a reference from a person's real name to the heading established using a nickname: Ogle, Arthur, see Ogle, Bud).[22]

For many persons who happen to be authors, the heading authority work will already have been done and the heading established in LCNAF. If LCNAF is the first or second source searched, the cost of local headings authority work for persons who are authors might be lower than before, when the LCNAF was not available and each entry had to be established locally.

For persons who are not authors, costs might increase. Headings for these names are not likely to have been established in LCNAF and are not likely to be found in bibliographic catalogs, but these sources must nevertheless be checked in the process of authority work. Worse, since these names might not fit the criteria for LCNAF entry, the same work must be repeated a second or even a third time before LCNAF entry is warranted. The policy gambles on the unlikelihood of recurrence (a presumption I will discuss later in this paper). This is not unlike the LC policy for minimal level cataloging, in which headings are established according to *AACR 2*, but without cross references and without determining relationships with other names.[23]

One difference between headings management authority work based on *AACR 2* and enhanced context authority work is the preference for "best known" form of name when it come to establishing an authorized heading. Each is similarly concerned to locate variants, although archivists have traditionally been most interested in "real" names and fullest forms. Each is similarly concerned with documenting the sources of forms found. However, traditional enhanced context authority work has not always resulted in the creation of anything equivalent to an authority record as commonly envisioned; in many cases a narrative in the archival finding aid provides the historical background, and the public catalog is the authority file. Archivists faced with creating LCNAF/NACO records may fume and sputter at the new overhead of specific documentation ("sources found"), although for headings established primarily on the basis of information found in archival materials, the prospect may not be as daunting as it first appears (Figure 1 contains examples of headings established at least in part from evidence in archival materials).

Searching for and documenting name usage in archival materials merely requires a little common sense and creative reading of the rules that relate to choice among forms found. As in any other authority work based on *AACR 2*, the goal is determining the "best known" form of name. Rather than relying on forms presented formally on title pages and the like, the archival cataloger looks for forms presented formally as signatures on letters or documents, or forms presented formally on letterheads, calling cards, business cards — any instruments persons might use to identify themselves to others. In many cases the cataloger must make intelligent guesses, following the policy of choosing either the latest name or the fullest form when it is otherwise impossible to determine the predominant name or form of name.[24]

It is not always understood that the extent of authority work done, whether for headings management or enhanced context, is almost always a matter of internal cataloging policy. There are rules for establishing headings (*AACR 2/APPM*), and there are rather general and permissive rules for context notes (*APPM*), but they do not say how long and how far the cataloger must search for the background evidence.

WHAT IS THE PROPER FUNCTION OF A HEADING? AUTHORITY WORK FOR CORPORATE NAMES

The actual process of authority work for corporate names is no different than for personal names, as described above, but process is not the only issue. Another is the effect of the *AACR 2* rules that deal with entry of subordinate bodies — restricting in many cases the display of intermediate levels of hierarchy in a heading.

When archivists take the Society of American Archivists' workshop, Library Standards for Archival Description, they are admonished that a heading is not an organization chart. The reminder is necessary because the traditional archival approach to corporate entities reflects the importance of administrative hierarchy (the "organization chart"). By showing functional relationships among subordinate units, the structure of an administrative hierarchy can be used

Figure 1

LCNAF records established using archival materials (among other sources)

Partial records (variable fields only)

100 10 $a Kellogg, Frank B. $q (Frank Billings), $d 1856-1937.

400 10 $w nna $a Kellogg, Frank Billings, $d 1856-1937

670 $a NUCMC data from N.J. Hist. Soc. for Schley, R. Papers, 1670-1969 $b (Frank B. Kellogg)

670 $a WWWA, 1897-1942 $b (Kellogg, Frank Billings, diplomat; sec. of state; b. Potsdam, N.Y., 1856; s. Asa F. and Abigail (Billings) K.; adm. to bar 1877; sec. of state in cabinet of Pres. Coolidge, 1925-1929; home: St. Paul, Minn.; d. 1937)

670     $a LC data base, 3-24-87 $b (hdg.: Kellogg, Frank

        Billings, 1856-1937; usage: Frank B. Kellogg)

110 20 $a Minnesota Public Health Conference.

410 20 $a American Public Health Association. $b Minnesota

        Public Health Conference

510 20 $w a $a Minnesota State Sanitary Conference

510 20 $w b $a Minnesota Public Health Association (1956-)

670     $a Its Records, 1947-1950 $b (Minnesota Public Health

        Conference)

670     $a Its Fourth Annual Meeting ... 1950: $b t.p.

        (Minnesota Public Health Conference)

FIGURE 1 (continued)

670 &a Minnesota Public Health Association. Governing
Council. Procedural manual, 1977-1978: $b p. 1-1
(1946, Minnesota Public Health Conference formed from
Minnesota Sanitary Conference; affiliated with
American Public Health Association; 1956, Minnesota
Public Health Conference ch. name to Minnesota Public
Health Association)

Fields emphasized show archival materials as source
documentation.

to predict topical or functional relationships among records produced by the agencies or units in the hierarchy, and it therefore provides the archivist and researcher the means to locate relevant records in the absence of detailed content analysis of the records.

The function of a name heading is to collocate materials of or about the entity named — and this it does. What archives also require, however, is a way to collocate materials of or about related entities, e.g., all administrative units subordinate to an agency, or a particular unit's "parent" or "grandparent" agencies, or all agencies performing similar functions. What is wanted is not only a name, but a context for the name, perhaps even a means of classification.

Even if it did place a name in its administrative hierarchy, as some do, a heading generally is not a good surrogate for an organization chart or an administrative history. It is simply too terse to represent the complex and fluid relationships in bureaucratic organizations. Nor is the current USMARC authority format, with its limited capacity for designating relationships among headings (essentially, relationships between earlier and later names), capable of communicating this complex data.

What needs to be preserved in the hierarchy of corporate names is the relationship of successive subordination (i.e., the form may not be relevant), and its place in time. Headings alone can't do it. Name authority records provide for links between earlier and later names. The agency history records of the Research Libraries Group (RLG) Government Records Project — essentially enhanced authority records disguised as bibliographic records (see Figure 2) — can describe the relationships.[25] In most other bibliographic records for archival materials, biographical and historical context data is included in notes.[26]

Choice of appropriate access points in bibliographic records often can help restore the apparent loss of information as a result of hierarchically abridged headings. For many archival materials created by a subordinate unit, it might be possible for a cataloger to justify an added entry for the parent body.

Another obstacle to archival acceptance of standard headings management authority work is the persistence in many institutions of time-honored naming conventions — for subordinate units within

Figure 2

RLG Government Records Project agency history record
(variable fields only, without added access points)

110 1 $a Minnesota. Dept. of Human Rights.

245 00 $a Agency history record.

545     $a The Department of Human Rights was created by a
        legislative action in 1967 which combined three
        existing agencies: the State Commission Against
        Discrimination, which was the enforcement agency for
        anti-discrimination legislation; the Governor's Human
        Rights Commission, which was the education component;
        and the Governor's Commission on the Status of Women,
        which was concerned with employment discrimination
        faced by women (Laws 1967 c897).

545    $b The legislature also created two advisory bodies
       to serve the department, a Board of Human Rights and
       an Advisory Committee on Women's Affairs, having
       fifteen members each (Laws 1967 c897 s17). The
       board's membership was increased to 24 in 1969. This
       board recommends programs and policies to the
       commission of human rights and also acts as an appeal
       board.

545    $b The commissioner of human rights formulates
       policies in accordance with the Minnesota State Act
       Against Discrimination (Laws 1967 c897). Resolution
       of discrimination charges is the primary function of
       the department, but public education, aimed at
       eliminating and preventing discrimination, is also an
       important part of the department's work. In addition
       the commission conducts, publishes, and distributes

FIGURE 2 (continued)

research studies; creates state and local advisory

committees to further the goals of the department;

and provides assistance to Indians and women in the

state of Minnesota, in planning and programming to

effectively serve their needs.

545    $b List of commissioners: Frank C. Kent, 1967-1970;

Conrad Balfour, 1970-1971; Samuel L. Richardson,

1971-1975; William L. Wilson, 1975-1978; Marilyn E.

Virgil McClure, 1979-1982; Irene Gomez Bethke, 1983;

Linda Johnson, 1984- .

a college or university, for example. Cross references could be used, but most likely they would have to be made in local catalogs or authority files only.

In some such cases creative (but reversible) use of local headings can help ease the transition. For example, when the Minnesota Historical Society converted its State Archives holdings information to *APPM/AACR 2* records in the Research Libraries Information Network (RLIN), it seemed desirable to retain the non-*AACR 2* agency name forms established primarily for the purpose of filing paper finding aids. So, when these records were edited for the RLIN file, the primary access points were established according to *AACR 2* (many were already present in LCNAF), and the "filing title" for each series was entered in a local field, identified also with a special subfield marker. These names can always be isolated and, if necessary, modified or deleted without affecting other headings.

Ordinarily, according to good authority control practice, name variations should be recorded as cross references in authority records, not as added entries in bibliographic records. In this case, however, there was not always a one-to-one correspondence between filing title heading and *AACR 2* form: filing title headings "Education Department: Division of Vocational Rehabilitation" and "Economic Security Department: Division of Vocational Rehabilitation" are represented by the same *AACR 2* form "Minnesota. Division of Vocational Rehabilitation."[27] Even if one-to-one correspondence had made such cross references logical in a local authority file, there would have been no way to link them to the RLIN bibliographic records.[28]

There are two important points here. First, when existing transitional catalogs do not incorporate cross references, authority work that is theoretically correct is operationally nullified. Second, when pursuing a theoretically incorrect course as a matter of expediency, it is best to preserve an option to reverse it later.

ENHANCED AUTHORITY WORK

While anything that can be said about the creation of conventional headings management authority records and the maintenance of authority files would apply equally to their use in archives, there is a growing tension concerning the content, structure, and function of enhanced context authority data. Is it the same as the familiar (at least to archivists) administrative history or biographical sketch? Does it look like an expanded LCNAF headings management record or something else entirely? How do users draw inferences from this information, and how do the inferences function in retrieval?

As I noted earlier, RLG has encouraged experimentation in the use of special agency history records in the RLIN bibliographic database, but that is unlikely to accommodate both approaches to authority work. Figures 2 and 3 illustrate the differences between a typical agency history and a typical authority record for that agency's name heading.

The Working Group on Standards for Archival Description[29] discussed the need for definition of *new types of authority records*. At present we identify and describe all types of bibliographic material (including archival collections as works of accumulation) in essentially one kind of bibliographic record; we identify persons, corporate bodies, places, and topical subjects in essentially one type of authority record. Headings management does not recognize a significant difference between the entities named: for each name there is an authorized heading with cross references and documentation of the sources that warrant the choice of heading and references.

Enhanced authority records for people, organizations, or places (for example) are likely to be considerably different. Besides names, people have interpersonal relationships, work or professional affiliations, geographical mobility; organizations have members or employees, administrative structure, powers, functions, places of activity or jurisdiction, the ability to restructure themselves; places are characterized by spatial and jurisdictional relationships. Tracing this multidimensional network of associations in a graphic as well as verbal syndetic structure would be the job of enhanced authority work.

CONCLUSION

Archival cataloging, in this transitional period, comprises two kinds of authority work. If descriptive records for archival materials are to function effectively in bibliographic networks or in more

Figure 3

LCNAF record (variable fields only)

110 10 $a Minnesota. $b Dept. of Human Rights.

410 10 $a Minnesota. $b Human Rights, Dept. of

410 10 $a Minnesota. $b Human Rights Dept.

550 0 $w nb $a Civil rights $z Minnesota

667     $a AACR 1 form: Minnesota. Dept. of Human Rights

670     $a Its Annual report ... 1967/68: $b t.p. (Department
        of Human Rights, State of Minnesota) p. iii (1967
        Minnesota Legislature created the Department of Human
        Rights as part of the executive branch of state
        government); 1972: t.p. (Human Rights Department) p.
        6 (Department of Human Rights)

broadly conceived cultural information systems, then authority work in archives must support headings management, the traditional focus of authority control. On the other hand, in order to support retrieval by inference on the basis of provenance, archivists provide biographical and administrative history information—the product of what I have termed enhanced context authority work.

Headings management authority work in archives, no less than in libraries, should conform with existing standards, even if that means relinquishing some local control and changing previous local practices. The changes can be made if several obstacles are overcome. A logical sequence of authority research can minimize the costs of authority work for persons and corporate bodies that have published. Appropriate interpretation of rules can make archivists more comfortable using archival sources for researching and documenting forms of names for persons who have not published. Procedures based on the assumption that relatively few name headings will recur might minimize the cost of authority work for most names. Archivists should finally acknowledge that a corporate name heading, no matter how faithfully it reproduces administrative hierarchy, is always a poor substitute for an organization chart or an administrative history—or linked authority files with good reference structures—and let headings be headings. Finally, some local practices, including naming conventions, can be preserved if they are absolutely required for archival control and user service.

Enhanced context authority work, which archivists have long known as the historical research component of description, may be changing. The concept of an enhanced context authority *record* is still new enough to lack supporting rules or data structures. Rules for biographical and historical notes in bibliographic records (see Figure 4) and slightly more specific guidelines for agency history records (see Figure 5) are meant for brief narrative descriptions, but if the real heart of enhanced authority control is in the syndetic structure of associations, perhaps unstructured narrative is not the best vehicle for enhanced authority data. Perhaps these associations should be recorded as a kind of reference, where both the object of the reference and the nature of the relationship are specified.

The archival profession very much needs to analyze and document how archival catalogs compare with traditional bibliographic catalogs, and how enhanced authority data supports retrieval.

Earlier I described a procedure for headings management authority work that gambles on the unlikelihood that names will recur. Research on the distribution of authors' names in general library catalogs indicates that a majority (60-70%) do occur only once.[30] But similiar research in a catalog of music sound recordings showed a much smaller percentage (47%) occur only once.[31] What kinds of distributions would be found in archival catalogs? Are published authors' names more likely also to occur in archival catalogs than nonauthors' names? How would archival catalogs compare with catalogs for published works in the same region, same topical subject area, etc.? Without this kind of analysis, it would be difficult to know the best policies for archival authority work.

How well does inference based on provenance data work in retrieval? Lytle's research showed that the "provenance method" for retrieval worked about as well as content indexing (though neither method was very good). But the syndetic structure that supported it was in the heads of the archivist-searchers in the form of knowledge about the functional responsibilities and administrative relationships among agencies. Would the provenance method work better if that knowledge (i.e., enhanced authority data) were translated into searchable authority files with explicit syndetic structure?

It has been suggested that some of the authority work now done by catalogers might be shifted to appropriately designed online catalog *systems* and their users. Research shows that many of the references in existing name authority records, especially those varying from the established heading only in fullness or word order, might be unnecessary if the catalog permitted keyword searching with right truncation.[32] Further, if these were the only references in an authority record, would that record be necessary at all? But in enhanced authority records, references for name variants would not be the only, and certainly not the most important, references. Authority records would be required for all persons or organizations represented.

Finally, archival catalogs are no different from any other catalogs in that they could benefit from improvement in the way that the

Figure 4

Excerpt from Archives, Personal Papers, and Manuscripts, 2nd
ed. (Chicago: Society of American Archivists, 1989)

1.7B1. Biographical/Historical note.

Record briefly any significant information on the
creator/author of the archival material required to make its
nature or scope clear. For persons this may include place of
birth and domicile, variant names, occupations (if relevant
to the materials), and significant accomplishments (if
reflected in the materials). Dates of birth and death may
also be given here. For corporate bodies, this may include
information on the functions, purpose, and history of the
body, its administrative hierarchy, and earlier, variant, or
successor names.

Example: Established in the War Department 3 Mar. 1865,
to supervise all activities relating to refugees and
freedmen and to assume custody of all abandoned or
confiscated lands or property. Abolished 10 June 1872,
and remaining functions transferred to the Freedman's
Branch, Office of the Adjutant General and after 1879, to
the Colored Troops Division of the Office of Adjutant
General.

Figure 5

Sample guidelines for agency administrative histories

These should be narratives that outline the
administrative history of the agency, including legislative
or executive authorization, enumeration and description of
functions and changes in functional jurisdiction;
significant name changes; make-up of boards and commissions;
names, functions, and dates of existence of administrative
divisions; names of department heads, superintendents,
commissioners, when available (in list form). -- Minnesota
Historical Society, ca. 1980

results of authority work of either type are used to help users navigate the catalogs.

NOTES

1. *Archives, Personal Papers, and Manuscripts*, 2nd ed. (Chicago: Society of American Archivists, 1989), v; Steven Hensen, "The Use of Standards in the Application of the AMC Format," *American Archivist* 49 (Winter 1986): 31-40.

2. A term borrowed from Kathleen Roe of the New York State Archives.

3. Barbara Tillet notes the recent growth of the literature on authority control, "Considerations for Authority Control in the Online Environment" in *Authority Control in the Online Environment: Considerations and Practices* (New York: Haworth Press, 1989), 5; volume also published as *Cataloging and Classification Quarterly* 9, no. 3 (1989).

4. For information on authority work in general see Robert H. Burger, *Authority Work: The Creation, Use, Maintenance, and Evaluation of Authority Records and Files* (Littleton, Colo.: Libraries Unlimited, 1985). For information on authority control in archives, see Jackie Dooley, "An Introduction to Authority Control for Archivists" in *Archives and Authority Control: Proceedings of a Seminar Sponsored by the Smithsonian Institution, October 27, 1987*, Archival Informatics Technical Report v. 2, no. 2 (Summer 1988), 5-18.

5. Burger, *Authority Work*, 32-37; see also Robert H. Burger, "Artificial Intelligence and Authority Control," *Library Resources & Technical Services* (October/December 1984): 337-45.

6. While the recording of contextual (biographical and historical) data is not new in archives, only in the last decade have archivists really begun to analyze how that data functions in information retrieval or to connect it with authority work. See Richard H. Lytle, "Intellectual Access to Archives: I. Provenance and Content Indexing Methods of Subject Retrieval," *American Archivist* 43 (Winter 1980): 64-75; and "Intellectual Access to Archives: II. Report of an Experiment Comparing Provenance and Content Indexing Methods of Retrieval," *American Archivist* 43 (Spring 1980): 191-207; Max Evans, "Authority Control: An Alternative to the Record Group Concept," *American Archivist* 49 (Summer 1986): 249-61; David Bearman, *Towards National Information Systems for Archives and Manuscript Repositories: The National Information Systems Task Force (NISTF) Papers, 1981-1984* (Chicago: Society of American Archivists, 1987), 63; David Bearman and Richard Szary, "Beyond Authorized Headings: Authorities as Reference Files in a Multi-Disciplinary Setting," *Authority Control Symposium*, Papers presented during the 14th Annual ARLIS/NA Conference, New York, N.Y., February 10, 1986, ed. by Karen Muller (Tucson, Ariz.: Art Libraries Society of North America, 1987), 69-78.

7. Using historical contextual information in retrieval is the "provenance indexing method" described by Lytle.

8. Rule 1.7B1 in *APPM*, second ed., (see figure 4) covers context information given in catalog records that contain descriptions of archival materials.

9. By integrated, I mean catalogs that contain bibliographic records for works in various presentation media (books, videorecordings, computer files) as well as records for materials subject to archival control.

10. The second edition of *Archives, Personal Papers, and Manuscripts* (*APPM*) includes rules, many drawn verbatim from *Anglo-American Cataloguing Rules*, 2nd ed. (*AACR 2*), for formulating headings for persons, corporate bodies, geographic names, and uniform titles.

11. Through NACO, catalogers at a number of libraries have been trained to create authority records for LCNAF, so it is really no longer *just* the Library of Congress Name Authority File.

12. *NUCMC* creates LCNAF records for names represented in *NUCMC* entries.

13. There are differing opinions on the role of local authority files, summarized in Arlene G. Taylor, "Research and Theoretical Considerations in Authority Control," in *Authority Control in the Online Environment*, 47-48.

14. The gap between principle and practice concerning references is illustrated in Joseph W. Palmer, "Subject Authority Control and Syndetic Structure — Myth and Realities: An Inquiry into Certain Subject Heading Practices and Some Questions about their Implications," *Cataloging and Classification Quarterly* 7 (Winter 1986): 71-95. Palmer's study of practices in the card catalogs of several libraries of Erie County, N.Y., showed that the smaller libraries used few "see" references and no "see also" references. Materials were often scattered among old and new headings with no references.

15. Either the *Name Authorities Cumulative Microform Edition* (1977-1986 cumulation, $265; annual subscription for 1989, $210); *CDMARC Names* (CD-ROM version, annual subscription for 1989, $375); or LCNAF online via OCLC or RLIN membership.

16. R. Bruce Miller does give some estimates of the cost of authority work in "Authority Control in the Network Environment" in *Authority Control: The Key to Tomorrow's Catalog*, ed. by Mary Ghikas (Phoenix, Ariz.: Oryx Press, 1982), 36-49.

17. Bearman, *Toward National Information Systems*, 63; Tillet, "Considerations," 7.

18. Hensen, "The Use of Standards," 37.

19. This notion of existential vs. bibliographic universe is used by Arnold S. Wajenberg, "A Cataloger's View of Authorship," in *The Conceptual Foundations of Descriptive Cataloging*, ed. by Elaine Svenonius (San Diego: Academic Press, Inc., 1989), 24.

20. This is based on policies developed at the Minnesota Historical Society, Division of Library and Archives.

21. This presumes the archives has a working relationship with a NACO participating institution. For a sample NACO workform, see Burger, *Authority Work*, 26-27.

22. The process at the Minnesota Historical Society is complicated by the fact that there are, at the time of this writing, three public catalogs to search: the manuscripts card catalog, the RLIN AMC database (for State Archives and for manuscripts cataloged after June 1988), and the library catalog in a PALS database. Authority work done for LCNAF/NACO at the appropriate level — here the state — is likely to benefit other cataloging agencies as well as the establishing agency.

23. Tillet, "Considerations," 8.

24. *APPM*, 2nd ed., rules 3.2A and 3.3A1.

25. In this project (an extension of the earlier Seven States Project) funded by the National Historical Records and Publications Commission (NHPRC), government archives have experimented with creating records for agency administrative histories separate from descriptions of archival materials. They reside in the Research Libraries Information Network (RLIN) bibliographic file, where they may be searched along with descriptions of archival materials created by those agencies.

26. Rule 1.7B1 in *APPM*, second ed., (see figure 4) covers context information given in catalog records that contain descriptions of archival materials.

27. The Division of Vocational Rehabilitation was transferred from one department to another. While the change might not affect the *AACR 2* form of name, it could affect the organization of the division's records and thus their archival control.

28. This example was also described in the author's "Authority Files in an Archival Setting" in *Archives and Authority Control*, Archival Informatics Technical Report v. 2, no. 2 (Summer 1988): 29-34.

29. This body of sixteen invited participants was convened under a grant from the National Historical Publications and Records Commission (NHPRC) to Harvard University as administrator. Larry Dowler of Harvard chaired the group, which met in December 1988 and June 1989; its final report is scheduled to be published in the *American Archivist* early in 1990.

30. See, especially William Gray Potter, "When Names Collide: Conflict in the Catalog and AACR 2," *Library Resources & Technical Services* 24 (Winter 1980): 3-16.

31. Arsen R. Papakhian, "The Freqency of Personal Name Headings in the Indiana University Music Library Card Catalogs," *Library Resources & Technical Services* 29 (July/September 1985): 273-285.

32. For example, Mark R. Watson and Arlene G. Taylor, "Implications of Current Reference Structures for Authority Work in Online Environments," *Information Technology and Libraries* (March 1987): 10-19.

Record Formatting:
MARC AMC

Lisa B. Weber

SUMMARY. This paper discusses how archivists use the MARC AMC format to exchange information about archival materials. The paper explains the modifications that MARC AMC introduced to the MARC bibliographic formats; gives examples of a record in generic USMARC AMC, RLIN AMC, and OCLC AMC; and considers the possible impact of format integration. The paper concludes with some thoughts about the changes that MARC AMC is causing in the archival profession.

INTRODUCTION

In *MARC for Library Use*, Walt Crawford states that "MARC is the single most important factor in the growth of library automation in the United States and other countries."[1] While it is still too early to tell whether the MARC (MAchine-Readable Cataloging)[2] format will have the same impact in the archival community, it appears that some sort of revolution is in the making. By all indications, the use of the MARC Format for Archival and Manuscripts Control (AMC) is changing the nature and practice of describing archival material.

The purpose of this paper is to discuss precisely how archivists

Lisa B. Weber is Assistant Director for Technological Evaluation, Records Program of the National Historical Publications and Records Commission. Previously, Ms. Weber held the position of Program Officer for Automation at the Society of American Archivists (SAA) where she developed and taught workshops on the MARC AMC format. She is the coauthor of *MARC for Archives and Manuscripts: A Compendium of Practice*, for which she received the C.F.W. Coker Prize. Ms. Weber was also awarded the 1989 Esther J. Piercy Award by the American Library Association's Association for Library Collections and Technical Services (formerly the Resources and Technical Services Division).

use the MARC AMC format to exchange descriptive information
about archival materials. To understand this practice, it is first necessary to briefly describe the MARC format in general and the
MARC AMC format specifically. Because some of the requirements for describing primary resource materials differ from those of
other library research materials, MARC AMC introduced a number
of significant changes to the format which are summarized. Examples of a MARC AMC record in three formats: generic, OCLC, and
RLIN, and a discussion of the MARC AMC fields used most often
follows. The paper concludes by considering the possible impact of
format integration and why the use of MARC AMC is fomenting
change in the archival profession.

WHAT IS MARC?

The MARC format is a standard method of identifying, organizing, and communicating information about materials found in libraries. Librarians began to develop the MARC format more than
twenty years ago to facilitate the computer exchange of catalog records. The format itself is composed of individual pieces of information called data elements. A data element is simply a category of
information such as title, date, or subject. The MARC format identifies data elements through the use of a labelling system of fields
and subfields. The MARC format is a standard structure that provides places for all the categories of information one needs to use to
describe materials to which libraries provide access.

The format is composed of several parts, each of which is intended to contain a particular kind of data. These parts are the
leader, record directory, and fields. Fields are either fixed or variable in length. Each field has a unique three digit identifying number called a tag, which labels the content of the field for computer
retrieval. Variable fields often contain subfields that are subdivisions of a field containing more specific information. Each subfield
is identified by a special subfield delimiter (represented in this paper as $) followed by an alpha or numeric character. Fields and
subfields are used to set off the data in a consistent manner so that
the information can be identified and retrieved. The format allows
many of the subfields and fields to be repeated within a single rec-

ord while others occur only once. The Library of Congress (LC) publishes the *USMARC Format for Bibliographic Data Including Guidelines for Content Designation*, which defines the format and is updated periodically when the format changes. The American Library Association's interdivisional MARBI committee advises the Library of Congress on additions and changes to the USMARC formats.

In fact, three separate MARC formats comprise the universe called MARC. They are the MARC formats for (1) bibliographic data,[3] (2) authority data,[4] and (3) holdings data.[5] Although currently in transition because of format integration, the MARC format for bibliographic data encompasses seven individual formats for different types of library materials. These are books; serial publications; visual materials (i.e., photographs, graphics, and moving images); music (both scores and sound recordings); maps; computer files; and archival and manuscript materials. This paper concentrates on MARC AMC, which is part of the bibliographic format. Archivists are just beginning to explore the use of the MARC formats for authority and holdings data.[6]

WHAT IS MARC AMC?

Archivists are relative newcomers in the use of the MARC format although the MARC format for Manuscripts was available as early as 1973. When the designers of MARC at the Library of Congress began their work over twenty years ago, the original intent was to develop one format to encompass all types of library materials. Practicality and time constraints, however, dictated that LC develop individual formats, the first one being the MARC format for books. In 1969, LC produced its first MARC formatted machine-readable tapes for English-language monographs.[7] Gradually adding other formats, LC issued the MARC format for Manuscripts in 1973. It never gained wide acceptance by the archival community because it failed to reflect archival concepts and needs. The fact that neither the *National Union Catalog of Manuscript Collections (NUCMC)* nor the Manuscript Division at the Library of Congress used it, testifies to its inadequacies.

Though archivists virtually ignored the MARC manuscripts format, they did not ignore using automated techniques to better manage their collections. In fact, many of the major, resource-rich archival institutions were busy developing in-house computer systems.[8] At the same time, archivists were interested in sharing information about their holdings. Providing better access to primary resource materials had long been a goal to which *NUCMC* and the National Historical Publications and Records Commission's (NHPRC) National Guide Project can attest. Observing the library community, archivists saw that the burgeoning national networks of OCLC (the Online Computer Library Center) and later, RLIN (the Research Libraries Information Network), were fueled by the economics of derivative cataloging. Most archivists reasoned that, since archival collections are, by definition, unique, they could not benefit from copy cataloging and therefore lacked the economic incentives to use MARC and to become part of library networks.[9]

Following that logic, it is somewhat surprising that archival repositories are today actively creating MARC records. How did this reversal occur? In 1977, the Society of American Archivists (SAA), appointed the National Information Systems Task Force (NISTF) to examine the issues surrounding its decision about which national information system (automated or not) to support. The two most likely candidates were *NUCMC* and the NHPRC's National Guide Project.[10] NISTF extricated itself from these highly political questions by focusing its energies on creating the "preconditions" for archival information exchange. What will come as no surprise to librarians is that fairly early during its deliberations, NISTF concluded that no single monolithic database could emerge as *the* national archival information system but rather that a national system would consist of "pieces" supported by a variety of institutions. To exchange information between these various pieces, the archival profession needed a common exchange format.

Given the archival community's reception of the MARC format for Manuscripts, NISTF was concerned that its choice of MARC as that exchange vessel would be controversial. NISTF, however, realized that the failure of the manuscripts format was not because of the MARC structure, but because of the inadequate definition of its elements. The task force recognized that using MARC would allow descriptions of archival and manuscript materials to be integrated with descriptions of other kinds of research materials held in libraries. NISTF also saw MARC as a cost-effective path to follow because large library bibliographic networks were already in place and able to support the format. Furthermore, although archivists could not gain the same economic benefits from copy-cataloging as the library community, NISTF envisioned the possibility of other kinds of exchanges that would have economic benefits including those derived from exchanges of authority and appraisal data.

NISTF understood that any exchange format needed to be built from the ground up and that the first step would be to define a set of data elements or categories of information collected, created, and generated by archivists, manuscripts curators, and records managers. Based on a study that verified NISTF's sense that the data elements were applicable to both archival and manuscript repositories, NISTF produced its data element dictionary.[11] The task force then had the job of fitting these data elements into the fields and subfields of the MARC format structure.

Actually, NISTF's task was not that simple because library and archival methodologies are not the same. Library and archival materials differ in method and intent of creation, as well as in the ways they come into custodial institutions. Consequently, these differences define the methods archivists use to control the materials. Archival materials are the unselfconscious products of daily functional activities resulting in collections or groups of materials. The guiding principles of archival control are provenance and life-cycle management. NISTF knew that to give the revised MARC format any chance of success, it would need to ensure that these fundamental archival principles could be accommodated by the format.

But why would the library community be willing to make major changes to something so economically successful and so critical to its current form of existence as the MARC format? The most obvious reason is that librarians realized that what are often referred to as the "family jewels" in repositories (personal papers of famous people or institutions) were missing from the bibliographic databases, despite their desired goal of integration of all library and research materials in one database. In support of this goal, the Research Libraries Group (RLG) committed itself to developing a format for archives and manuscripts that could be integrated with its existing database.[12] Additionally, several instrumental people wanted to incorporate archival exchange into the format and would prove useful allies.[13] Thus NISTF was able to introduce several entirely new concepts into the body of the MARC format, expand or revise several library practices that were already in place, and inaugurate a new political alliance previously unknown to MARC and the library community.

New Concepts

MARC AMC introduced major innovations. First, NISTF created a format that is not media-specific like the other MARC formats, because archival and manuscript materials are not a media type like books, maps or music. A key distinguishing element of the MARC AMC format is that it is an approach to description and can be used to describe groupings or collections of different formats of material — paper, microforms, photographs, sound recordings, data files — that are typical of archival collections. Moreover, the format can be used to describe any archival unit at any level and is not bound in a rigid hierarchy, because NISTF found that most of the data elements in its dictionary were not level-dependent. Although most archivists use MARC AMC to describe at the collection or series level, the format can also be used to describe record groups, subseries, or even items.

Second, NISTF recognized that the format had to accommodate the concept of control over archival processes or actions that are performed upon the records themselves because, as archivists know, actions affect the actual content of the materials in intellectually significant ways. Because collections change over time, archivists require integration, not segregation, of intellectual/descriptive control from administrative/management control. This concept was quite foreign to the library community. There, the focus is on descriptive control only and the creation of a catalog or MARC record that rarely changes. Instead of creating a separate field in the format for each kind of administrative action, process, or activity that an archivist needs to record, those designing the AMC format suggested a self-defining "action" field that allows archivists to record any action that is important to associate with the description of the materials. The action field, 583, embodies the concept of control in the AMC format.

The third new concept that AMC introduced to the MARC formats is that of "intra-record links," the ability to define some smaller portion of the unit being described. Within the context of a collection description, archivists need to be able to specify certain portions of the whole collection, series, or group. For example, it is not uncommon for only part of a record group to have restrictions on access or for certain parts of a collection to need special conservation treatment. Subfield $3, entitled "materials specified," allows the archivist to restrict the applicability of the field to some portion of the record — to the materials specified. Subfield $3 allows archivists to isolate or emphasize parts of the record in the context of the whole.[14]

Extended or Revised Practice

In addition to introducing major innovations, NISTF needed to expand or revise several practices already embodied in the MARC formats to enable archivists to adequately describe archival materials. Note fields (the 5xx block) is one such area. In library cataloging, notes are considered optional and used primarily to clarify information contained in other parts of the records. Many library catalog records do not contain note fields, but when they do, librarians most often put them in the generalized note field 500. For archivists, multiple and often complex notes are the heart of the entry. NISTF defined six new note fields for AMC and "borrowed" six more from other formats. AMC records are often long, due in part to the extensive use of multiple note fields in individual records.

A second, and more significant expansion to MARC practice is the wholehearted acceptance of item-specific data in the format.[15] Since derivative or copy-cataloging is the motivation behind MARC, the formats were designed to contain data that is applicable to all copies of the bibliographic item in order to provide "generic" catalog records to which libraries can add institution-specific descriptive information. Of course, the exact opposite is true for archival materials. Given their unique nature, virtually all data is collection or item-specific. Although the MARC bibliographic formats could already accommodate some local data within narrow confines, defining AMC to completely accept item-specific data was a leap that librarians were willing to make for the sake of incorporating descriptions of archival and manuscript materials in the data bases.

NISTF was not always able to convince the library community of adaptations it wanted to make to the format. For example, the task force understood that the distinctions librarians make between subject and added entries were not transferable to the archival community. Archivists are confronted with deciding in which field to put names of correspondents. Librarians distinguish between people involved in the creation of the work (authors and editors) and people represented in the work (subject). But are correspondents additional creators, subjects, or both? One can argue that a letter by a person reveals as much about that person. In an attempt to circumvent this issue, NISTF proposed a number of "index term" fields including ones for personal name, corporate name, topic or event, geopolitical or geophysical entity, occupation, form, genre, and function. The approved AMC format retains the library distinction between creator and subject, combines the concepts of form and genre, and adds a field for physical characteristics access (originated in the visual materials community). NISTF was successful in introducing two new fields for access points: field 656, "Index term — Occupation," and 657, "Index term — Function."

A New Political Alliance

One important innovation that MARC AMC introduced to the MARC formats concerns a political rather than technical issue. Because archivists viewed the original MARC format for manuscripts as unsatisfactory and were both wary and reluctant to give control of this new exchange structure to a group outside the profession, NISTF negotiated an understanding of joint ownership of MARC AMC between the Library of Congress and the Society of American Archivists. With SAA Council's approval, NISTF disbanded itself in 1983 and was succeeded by the Committee on Archival Information Exchange (CAIE). CAIE's responsibilities include maintaining the data element dictionary and the MARC AMC format. A member of CAIE acts as liaison to the MARBI committee.

THE MARC AMC RECORD

MARC AMC records are different from most other MARC bibliographic records in a number of ways. The most obvious variation is length. AMC records frequently include numerous and often extensive note fields that provide information about the content, provenance or context, physical aspects, and access to the materials. The large number of access points also contribute to the length of AMC records. The RLIN database contains many records that have over one hundred added entry fields.[16] At the same time, AMC records use very few coded fields.

There are two other aspects of AMC records that are not apparent at first glance, but also contribute to the differences between AMC and most other kinds of bibliographic records. The first is that AMC records are usually not used for copy cataloging.[17] Unlike the library community, which must focus on creating and distributing easily distinguishable catalog records so that databases do not include multiple entries for the same item, archivists are creating MARC records for unique material. This does not mean, however, that archivists should only think about their own descriptive needs. MARC AMC records must integrate into national and local library databases as well. The other aspect that differentiates AMC cataloging is the changing nature of the records. Because archivists are interested in controlling archival materials, AMC records are often updated and revised over time.

Figure 1 is an example of a generic MARC AMC record.[18] Figures 2 and 3 are examples of the same record in the RLIN AMC and OCLC AMC formats. Figure 4 is a table including the fields used most often in the description of archival materials. The form or content of the fields is determined by standards other than MARC AMC, such as *The Anglo-American Cataloging Rules (AACR2)* and *Archives, Personal Papers, and Manuscripts (APPM)*, and various controlled vocabulary lists including the *Library of Congress Subject Headings* and the *Art and Architecture Thesaurus*. Discussions

FIGURE 1. Generic USMARC AMC Record for a Manuscript Collection

LEADER		0000ßbcßß2200000ßaß4500
001		$aCTYV84-A445
008		840509i18981986ctußßßßßßßßßßßßßßßßßßengßd
040		$aCtY$cCtY$eaapm
100	1	$aAcheson, Dean,$d1893-1971.
245	00	$aDean Gooderham Acheson papers,$f1898-1986.
300		$a37$flinear ft.$a(75$fboxes)
351		$aArranged in five series: I. General Correspondence, 1910-1971. II. Correspondence Concerning Speeches and Writings, 1936-1972. III. Speeches and Writings, 1901-1978. IV. Miscellaneous Files, ca. 1898-1972. V. 1985 Additions, 1919-1969.
545		$aLawyer, author, Secretary of State in the Truman administration, and member of the Yale Corporation.$bBorn on April 11, 1893 in Middletown, Connecticut, Acheson attended Groton, Yale College and Harvard Law School. He clerked for Supreme Court Justice Louis Brandeis before joining the ...*
520		$aPapers include correspondence, writings, speeches, memoranda, and photographs, documenting Dean Acheson's life after leaving the U.S. State Department in 1953. Also documented is his work as a member of the Yale Corporation and his long friendship with Felix Frankfurter, Archibald MacLeish, and others. The correspondence and memoranda contain Acheson's views on many contemporary issues in America foreign policy such as Korea, the Middle East, NATO, Germany, the war in Vietnam, and South Africa. The papers also include Acheson's later reflections on his years in public life and assessments of the U.S. government under the Kennedy, Johnson, and Nixon administrations ...*
541		$aAcheson, David$cgift$d1981-1988.

*Remainder of the field omitted.

FIGURE 1 (continued)

506		$3William S. Lewis and Archibald MacLeish files$arestricted until 1995,
506		$3Correspondence in box 70$arestricted until 2020.
506		$3Eugene V. Rostow files in box 71$arestricted during the lifetime of Rostow or until his papers in the Manuscripts and Archives Department are opened.
506		$3Classified documents in the Security File$arestricted until declassified by government.
555		$aUnpublished finding aid in repository.
524		$aDean Gooderham Acheson Papers. Manuscripts and Archives, Yale University Library.
544		$dAssociated material: Dean Acheson's public papers are housed in the$aHarry S. Truman Library, Independence, Missouri.
600	10	$aAcheson, Dean,$d1893-1971.
600	10	$aAcheson, David C.
600	10	$aAdenauer, Konrad,$d1876-1967.
655	7	$aPhotoprints.$2ftamc
656	7	$aDiplomats.$21csh
656	7	$aJournalists.$21csh
...*		
851		$aManuscripts and Archives,$bYale University Library,$cBox 1603A Yale Station, New Haven, CT 06520.

*A number of 600, 610, 650, 651, and 656 fields are omitted.

of the use of the fields by the first MARC AMC practitioners can be found in *MARC For Archives and Manuscripts: A Compendium of Practice* and a recent article by Janet Gertz and Leon Stout.[19] The newly revised edition of *APPM*[20] also includes examples of MARC-tagged fields. Additionally, the bibliographic networks of OCLC,

FIGURE 2. RLIN MARC AMC Record for a Manuscript Collection

```
ID:CTYV84-A445  RTYP:d    ST:p          MS:    EL:      AD:05-09-84
CC:9554  BLT:bc  DCF:a    CSC:d   MOD:  PROC:b          UD:03-06-89
PP:ctu     L:eng  PC:i     PD:1898/1986  REP:
MMD:       OR:  POL:  DM:    RR:      COL:  EML:  GEN:  BSE:
```

040		CtY$cCtY$eaapm
100	1	Acheson, Dean,$d1893-1971.
245	00	Dean Gooderham Acheson papers,$f1898-1986.
300		37$flinear ft.$a(75$fboxes)
351		Arranged in five series: I. General Correspondence, 1910-1971. II. Correspondence Concerning Speeches and Writings, 1936-1972. III. Speeches and Writings, 1901-1978. IV. Miscellaneous Files, ca. 1898-1972. V. 1985 Additions, 1919-1969.
545		Lawyer, author, Secretary of State in the Truman administration, and member of the Yale Corporation.$bBorn on April 11, 1893 in Middletown, Connecticut, Acheson attended Groton, Yale College and Harvard Law School. He clerked for Supreme Court Justice Louis Brandeis before joining the ...*
520		Papers include correspondence, writings, speeches, memoranda, and photographs, documenting Dean Acheson's life after leaving the U.S. State Department in 1953. Also documented is his work as a member of the Yale Corporation and his long friendship with Felix Frankfurter, Archibald MacLeish, and others. The correspondence and memoranda contain Acheson's views on many contemporary issues in America foreign policy such as Korea, the Middle East, NATO, Germany, the war in Vietnam, and South Africa. The papers also include Acheson's later reflections on his years in public life and assessments of the U.S. government under the Kennedy, Johnson, and Nixon administrations ...*

*Remainder of the field omitted.

FIGURE 2 (continued)

506    $3William S. Lewis and Archibald MacLeish files$arestricted until
       1995.

506    $3Correspondence in box 70$arestricted until 2020.

506    $3Eugene V. Rostow files in box 71$arestricted during the lifetime
       of Rostow or until his papers in the Manuscripts and Archives
       Department are opened.

506    $3Classified documents in the Security File$arestricted until
       declassified by government.

555   Unpublished finding aid in repository.

524   Dean Gooderham Acheson Papers. Manuscripts and Archives, Yale
       University Library.

544    $dAssociated material: Dean Acheson's public papers are housed in
       the$aHarry S. Truman Library, Independence, Missouri.

600 10   Acheson, Dean,$d1893-1971.

600 10   Acheson, David C.

600 10   Adenauer, Konrad,$d1876-1967.

655   7   Photoprints.$2ftamc

656   7   Diplomats.$2lcsh

656   7   Journalists.$2lcsh

...*

851   Manuscripts and Archives,$bYale University Library,$cBox 1603A
       Yale Station, New Haven, CT 06520.

Archival Control Segment

RPGN   MS 25

MATL   Papers

SRCE   Acheson, David, 1981-1988.

PLOC   AV 38a1-9 (75 archive)

*Ninety-three 600, 610, 650, 651, and 656 fields omitted.

FIGURE 2 (continued)

```
ACT        Proj. cat.

TAC        02/15/84

AGT        1a

ACT        Restriction review

TAC        06/30/85

AGT        nlf

...**
```

**A number of process control segments are omitted.

RLIN, and the Western Library Network (WLN) provide their own documentation for the use of the MARC AMC fields in their respective systems.

Summary of Figures

Some of the differences between the generic USMARC AMC format and those of RLIN and OCLC are represented in figures 1-3. The distinctions result from the manner in which OCLC and RLIN implement the USMARC AMC format. These differences fall into five categories: length, display conventions, indexing capabilities, reporting capabilities and functional requirements. It must also be remembered that some users download RLIN and OCLC records into local library systems that impose different system requirements and limitations. The requirements of these local library systems also influence the coding of MARC AMC records.

Length

One of the most obvious differences between the two systems is the size of the record. The maximum length of an OCLC record is 4k or 4096 characters, approximately four screens on a video display terminal. Moreover, the maximum size of any one field in an OCLC record is 1,230 characters. Additionally, an OCLC record

FIGURE 3. OCLC MARC AMC Record for a Manuscript Collection

OCLC: 6004045   Rec stat: c Entrd: 840509   Used: 890306

Type: b   Bib lvl: c   Lang: eng   Source: d

Repr: Enc lvl: I Ctry: ctu   Dat tp: i

Desc: a   Mod rec: Dates: 1898.1986

1 040   YUS $c YUS

2 090 $b

3 049   NARA

4 100 1   Acheson, Dean, $d 1893-1971.

5 245 00   Papers, $f 1898-1986.

6 260 $c

7 300   37 linear ft.

8 351   Arranged in five series and addition: I. General Correspondence,
             1910-1971. II. Correspondence Concerning Speeches and Writings,
             1936-1972. III. Speeches and Writings, 1901-1978. IV.
             Miscellaneous Files, ca. 1898-1972. V. 1983 Additions, 1010
             1969.

9 545   Lawyer, author, Secretary of State in the Truman administration,
             and member of the Yale Corporation. $b Born on April 11, 1893 in
             Middletown, Connecticut, Acheson attended Groton, Yale College and
             Harvard Law School. He clerked for Supreme Court Justice Louis
             Brandeis before joining the ...*

10 520   Papers include correspondence, writings, speeches, memoranda, and
             photographs, documenting Dean Acheson's life after leaving the
             U.S. State Department in 1953. Also documented is his work as a
             member of the Yale Corporation and his long friendship with Felix
             Frankfurter, Archibald MacLeish, and others...*

11 541   Acheson, David $c gift $d 1981-1988.

*Remainder of the field omitted.

FIGURE 3 (continued)

12	506	$3 William S. Lewis and Archibald MacLeish files $a restricted until 1995.
13	506	$3 Correspondence in box 70 $a restricted until 2020.
14	506	$3 Eugene V. Rostow files in box 71 $a restricted during the lifetime of Rostow or until his papers in the Manuscripts and Archives Department are opened.
15	506	$3 Classified documents in the Security File $a restricted until declassified by government.
16	555	Unpublished finding aid in repository.
17	524	Dean Gooderham Acheson Papers. Manuscripts and Archives, Yale University Library.
18	544	$d Associated material: Dean Acheson's public papers are housed in the $a Harry S. Truman Library, Independence, Missouri.
19	583	Project Cataloged $c 02-15-84 $k 1a
20	583	Restrictions Review $c 06-30-85 $k n1f
21	650	0 Presidents $z United States.
22	650	0 Diplomacy.
23	650	0 German reunification question (1949-)
24	655	7 Photoprints. $2 ftamc
25	656	7 Diplomats. $2 lcsh
26	656	7 Journalists. $2 lcsh
27	700	10 Acheson, Dean, $d 1893-1971.
28	700	10 Acheson, David C.
29	700	10 Adenauer, Konrad, $d 1876-1967.

...*

*Eleven 600, 610, 651, 700, and 710 fields omitted.

FIGURE 4. MARC AMC Fields Often Used to Describe Archival Materials

FIELD	TITLE	DESCRIPTION
Leader/06	Type of Record	b= AMC
Leader/07	Bibliographic Level	c= Collection
Leader/18	Descriptive Cataloging Form	a= Records described according to APPM are coded "a."
008/06	Type of Date Code	i= Inclusive dates
008/07-14	Date 1 and Date 2	The inclusive dates of the collection.
010	Library of Congress Control	*NUCMC* number or numbers.
1xx	Main entry	The creator of the materials.
245	Title Statement	Titles are most often supplied by the catalogers and frequently composed of several part: the main entry, the form of material, and the inclusive dates of the collection. Subfields for these and additional components comprise field 245.
300	Physical Description	For those archivists who want to count or track statistics, numbers are subfielded separately from units of measurement.
351	Organization and Arrangement	Subfields enable archivists to make the distinction between organization--the manner in which the collection as a whole is subdivided into smaller units--and arrangement--the pattern of arrangement of materials (i.e. alphabetical, chronological,

FIGURE 4 (continued)

		numerical) within the unit described. Archivists can also indicate the hierarchical position of the described materials relativ to other records with the same provenance ($c, archival level).
5xx	Note fields block	Although the MARC AMC format provides the opportunity for detailed content designation throug the numerous available fields and subfields, not all repositories choose this approach. The decision depends upon the repository's system implementation and local needs.
53x	Microform and other reproduction notes	Fields 530, 533, and 535 are used to record information about materials that have been microformed or otherwise reproduced.[21]
545	Biographical or historical note	Information about the individual or corporate body that created the materials.
520	Summary note	The most important part of the record, provides a narrative description of the scope and contents of the materials.
541	Immediate source of acquisition note	The donor or source of the materials.
561	Provenance note	The history of the materials prior to the time of acquisition.

506	Restriction on access note	Any restriction imposed on access to the materials.
540	Terms governing use and reproduction note	Information about the terms governing the use of the materials after access has been provided.
555	Finding aid note	Identifying administrative and intellectual controls over the described materials.
524	Preferred citation of described materials note	Format for the citation of the archival materials preferred by the custodian.
544	Location of associated materials note	The custodian of materials related by provenance to the materials being described.
580	Linking entry complexity note	The description of a component part tied to the next larger unit in the collection. Field 580 is always found in the subordinate record in the hierarchy.
773	Host item entry	The field that provides the machine-link between the host and component records, e.g. between a collection and series.
600	Subject added entry-personal name	Archivists who believe that the writer of the letter is also the subject of the letter, enter correspondents in the 600 field.

FIGURE 4 (continued)

610	Subject added entry-corporate name	Corporate bodies represented in the materials.
650	Subject added entry-topical heading	Subjects represented in the materials.
651	Subject added entry-geographic name	Geographic place names represented in the materials.
655	Index term-genre/form	Genre and/or form terms represented in the materials.
656	Index term-occupation	Occupations reflected in the described materials.
657	Index term-function	Term that describes the activity or function that generated the described materials.
7xx	Added entries	Most often used for additional creators
851	Location	Location of the custodian of the materials.

cannot contain more than fifty variable fields, nor can OCLC's catalog card print program accommodate more than 30 printing fields within a tag group (i.e., 6xx or 7xx). RLIN has more flexible limits to its overall record size and the maximum size of a record is far greater than that of OCLC. A single RLIN field is limited to one screen, although field repeatability allows for extensive description. Moreover, RLIN records have no limits on the number of fields in a record. The limit to the total size of the record is between 29k and 32k or up to 32,768 characters. Because AMC records tend to be lengthy and have multiple note fields and numerous added entry fields, the size and field limits to OCLC records can be troublesome for catalogers describing archival materials.

Display Conventions

Apparent from the figures, RLIN and OCLC use different fixed field mnemonic codes. In both cases, however, these codes are derived from the leader and field 008 in the generic record. RLIN has several kinds of online display formats in addition to the MARC-tagged display; OCLC does not. Some of the display constants, standard labels used to introduce information in a field, also vary between the two systems.

Indexing Capabilities

RLIN and OCLC have different online indexing capabilities which sometimes result in archivists choosing different fields to hold the data. The most obvious case is the choice between entering the names of correspondents into the 600 or 700 fields. In addition to the philosophical differences, OCLC users have been faced with a system that does not index information contained in any 6xx field. Therefore, it has been more attractive to put names of correspondents into the 700 fields and have online retrieval access to them. RLIN users have online retrieval access to both the 600 and the 700 fields. To circumvent the philosophical problem of which category to choose, RLIN indexes all names in the 6xx block twice, by subject and by name. The result is that most RLIN users put names of correspondents in the 600 field whereas OCLC users put the names in the 700 field. With OCLC's implementation of the EPIC system, many of its searching limitations for references purposes will be alleviated.

Reporting Capabilities

RLIN produces cards as well as other kinds of products such as guides and administrative reports. OCLC only produces card sets. Many of the note fields do not print on OCLC catalog cards, sometimes forcing catalogers to not use the appropriate note fields because of the need to have the notes print on cards.

Functional Requirements

As discussed earlier, the AMC format introduced the concept of control into the MARC formats which is embodied in field 583 (Actions). In OCLC, the institution that enters the record may enter data into the 583 field, like other note fields, but the field is only displayed to the inputting institution. To others viewing the same OCLC AMC record, the 583 field and data contained within it is masked. To accommodate the concept of control, RLG enhanced its software and created the Archival Control Segment (ARC). The ARC segment is composed of AMC fields 583, 541 (Immediate Source of Acquisition note), and several local RLIN fields, all of which are represented by mnemonic codes. The segment, attached to the bibliographic portion of the record, contains donor and administrative control information. The inputting institution can choose if it wants others to see the information in the ARC segment. Archival repositories use the information to generate many kinds of administrative reports.

Figure 4 identifies the fields most often used in MARC AMC records. In addition to the numerous note fields, the table also shows the multiple categories of index terms including those added to the MARC format for the AMC community such as function and occupation.

FORMAT INTEGRATION

In June, 1989, the MARBI committee formally accepted the proposal for format integration — the seven USMARC formats for bibliographic data are being integrated into one single format. Although the implementation of format integration by LC, OCLC, and RLG will not be completed until the end of 1993, the result will be that all fields within the MARC bibliographic formats will be available to describe any type of material. In theory, format integration should enable catalogers of all types of materials to improve existing practice. An integrated format will provide for full description of an item that has more than one form aspect such as a book issued with a music cassette. It should also solve one of the most difficult questions for archivists of "which format to use" when faced with describing collections that are comprised of one medium such as historical photographs, moving images or computer files. Nevertheless, because of the basic structure of the format, this might not be the case.

The format integration proposal identified two general descriptive perspectives embodied in the MARC formats: the control aspects (namely serial and archival control) and the form aspects (namely textual [books and periodicals], maps, music, visual materials, and computer files). The proposal facilitated the control aspects for all forms of material by allowing the associated data elements to be described for each form. The reasons format integration will not solve the "which format to use" question lie in the definition of two leader bytes that are used to express three separate concepts: type of material, ways of handing material, and bibliographic level. Leader byte 06 (titled "Type of Record") includes codes for language material, music, projected media, sound recordings, etc. *and* a way of handling materials, namely archival and manuscript control. Leader byte 07 (entitled "Bibliographic Level") combines aspects of levels such as collection, subunit, and component part with a way of handling material, namely seriality. In essence, the MARC format treats archival and manuscript control as a type of material.[22]

The format actually embodies three, not two, control aspects, the third being bibliographic control or item cataloging. A simple and elegant solution would be to define a separate character position for type of control and include codes for each of the three aspects, thus explicitly recognizing the three ways of controlling materials currently supported by the MARC format: bibliographic control, serial control, and archival and manuscript control. LC and MARBI are aware of this possibility and are currently examining the implications of removing the code for AMC in Leader byte 06 and defining a new position in the leader for type of control. If they choose this solution, the MARC format for bibliographic data will be able to handle all types of control in a much more efficient and effective manner.

The most visible format integration battle for archivists centered around the inclusion of local data in MARC bibliographic records. Concurrent with the development of the MARC AMC format,

MARBI was also developing the MARC format for holdings, an exchange structure to contain information about the specific items a library holds as opposed to the bibliographic formats, which contain generic, not copy-specific data. NISTF had concluded that it did not want to use the holdings format because archives do not have holdings in the same sense that libraries do. NISTF also determined the need for an eye-readable (not coded) field that contained the repository location of the material described in the records so that a user, finding the record in a national or regional data base, could immediately know where the material was housed. MARBI approved the location field 851 in January of 1984 but changed its mind four years later and made the field obsolete in the integrated format, substituting the holdings field 852 (Location/Call Number) instead. Although the archival profession vigorously opposed this decision, archivists will be required to use holdings field 852 when format integration is implemented.

The results of the process of integrating the formats is of major significance to the archival community. The library community closely scrutinized archival practice because format integration makes the revolutionary concepts introduced to the MARC format by the archival community available to everyone. It appears that, at least in the beginning, system implementation of format integration will be transparent to the users. How systems implement the more revolutionary aspects of MARC AMC for other types of media remains unclear.

CONCLUSION

The revolutionary changes that MARC AMC is fostering in the archival community are reflected on two fronts. First, the development of the format and the subsequent computer system implementations have required archivists to think more systematically about how archival work is carried out. This has led to more sophisticated and refined archival methods and techniques.[23] The second change is occurring in the area of standards for archival description. Although the MARC AMC format is a structure for exchanging information, the format has forced the archival profession to confront its practices for describing archival materials. The uniqueness of archival materials has long been an excuse to perpetuate the profession's idiosyncratic descriptive practices. The archival profession traditionally has balked at rigorously examining archival description, let alone developing and using archival descriptive standards. But the widespread use of the format has demonstrated that archivists want to exchange information. It has also underscored the fact that to exchange data in a meaningful way, archivists need to follow standards for the construction of the content of the records describing archival materials as well as use of a standard structure. In response to the need for the archival profession to confront a number of descriptive standards issues, a Working Group on Standards for Archival Description recently convened and developed a set of recommendations for the profession.[24] The MARC AMC is fomenting an exciting revolution that is swiftly moving the profession ahead in its mission to provide better access to materials deemed archival.

NOTES

1. Crawford, Walt. *MARC for Library Use: Understanding Integrated US-MARC*, 2nd ed. Boston: G.K. Hall, 1989, p. 1. For a thorough discussion of the USMARC formats, consult this newly revised text.

2. MARC is an acronym derived from MAchine-Readable Cataloging and is a generic term applied to the universe of MARC formats. USMARC (United States MARC) refers to the set of options and content designations that are used by the Library of Congress. The terms USMARC or MARC are also applied to the MARC extensions such as OCLC MARC and RLIN MARC.

3. *USMARC Format for Bibliographic Data: Including Guidelines for Content Designation*. Washington, DC: Library of Congress, 1988.

4. *USMARC Format for Authority Data: Including Guidelines for Content Designation*. Washington, DC: Library of Congress, 1987.

5. *USMARC Format for Holdings and Locations: Including Guidelines for Content Designation*. Washington, DC: Library of Congress, 1984.

6. See Weber, Lisa B. "The 'Other' USMARC Formats: Authorities and Holdings; Do We Care to be Partners in this Dance, Too?" *The American Archivist*, 53 (Winter 1990) Forthcoming.

7. Avram, Henriette D. *MARC: Its History and Implications*. Washington, DC: Library of Congress, 1975, pp. 7-9.

8. Hickerson, H. Thomas. *Archives and Manuscripts: An Introduction to Automated Access*. Chicago: Society of American Archivists, 1981.

9. Bearman, David. "Archival and Bibliographic Information Networks." In *Archives and Library Administration: Divergent Traditions and Common Con-*

cerns, edited by Lawrence J. McCrank, pp. 99-110. New York: Haworth Press, 1986.

10. For discussions of the work of NISTF see Lytle, Richard H. "An Analysis of the Work of the National Information Systems Task Force." *The American Archivist, 47* (Fall 1984): 357-365; Sahli, Nancy. "Interpretation and Application of the AMC Format." *The American Archivist, 49* (Winter 1986): 9-20; Bearman, David. *Towards National Information Systems for Archives and Manuscript Repositories: The National Information Systems Task Force (NISTF) Papers 1981-1984*. Chicago: Society of American Archivists, 1987; and Hickerson, H. Thomas. "Archival Information Exchange and the Role of Bibliographic Networks." *Library Trends 36* (Winter 1988): 553-571.

11. The data element dictionary can be found in Sahli, Nancy. *MARC for Archives and Manuscripts: The AMC Format*. Chicago: Society of American Archivists, 1985.

12. "AMC Offers New Access to Nation's Archival Resources." *The Research Libraries Group News*, (September 1984), pp. 3-5.

13. Bearman, *Towards National Information Systems*. p. 7.

14. Field 773 already existed in the format to accommodate links between two separate archival records. For example, 773 enables a series to be linked to a collection description.

15. Subfield $5 (Institution to which field applies) and the MARC holdings format contain information that is specific to an individual repository.

16. Crawford, *MARC for Library Use*, p. 140.

17. The most obvious exception to this is microfilm reproductions of entire collections.

18. The example used in all three formats is based on an RLIN record which was put into the database by the Manuscript and Archives Department, Yale University Library. The author has taken the liberty of changing the record to illustrate certain features of the MARC AMC format.

19. Evans, Max J. and Weber, Lisa B. *MARC for Archives and Manuscripts: A Compendium of Practice*. Madison: State Historical Society of Wisconsin, 1985; Gertz, Janet and Stout, Leon J. "The MARC Archival and Manuscripts Control (AMC) Format: A New Direction in Cataloging." *Cataloging and Classification Quarterly, 9* (1989).

20. Hensen, Steven L. *Archives, Personal Papers, and Manuscripts*, 2nd ed. Chicago: Society of American Archivists, 1989.

21. Weber, Lisa B. "Describing Microforms and the MARC Formats: A Discussion Paper." *Archives and Museum Informatics, 1* (Summer 1987): 9-13.

22. When NISTF agreed to use Leader/06 for AMC, it was specifically defined as the way of handling material and not a type of material. The definition has been changed.

23. NISTF's development of AMC has resulted in the profession's experimenting with expanding the concept of authority files, exchanging appraisal data, and developing vocabularies for function and form of material. The Research Libraries Group's Seven State Project and Government Records Project, both

funded by the National Historical Publications and Records Commission, have taken the lead in all of these developments.

24. The recommendations and working papers developed by the Working Group on Archival Descriptive Standards, funded by the National Historical Publications and Records Commission, will be published in *The American Archivist*, *52* (Fall 1989).

The Automation Odyssey: Library and Archives System Design Considerations

Kathleen D. Roe

SUMMARY. This paper considers the issues and concerns relating to the integration of archival and manuscripts records into library systems, and how those systems can be used to support archival functions. Factors of importance in system design include: the differences in the nature of library and archival materials; the functions undertaken by libraries and archives, especially bibliographic control and retrieval; and varying library and archival needs for authority control and holdings/location information. Reasons to pursue shared systems, and issues for further action are also considered.

Librarians and archivists face serious constraints in their journey toward a fully automated environment. Technology at times takes on characteristics of the Siren's call to those involved in automated library and archives systems. The news media reports an astounding rate of technological development bordering on wizardry. Yet the technologies available to libraries and archives are generally not on the cutting-edge; in fact, they often are less sophisticated than those commonly available for more economically fruitful business applications. Economic constraints also make it unlikely that libraries and archives can create systems "hand-tailored" to their specific needs, so instead must make adjustments to operate with off-the-shelf software. Librarians have faced this problem for several decades, and various automated library systems are available ranging

Kathleen D. Roe is Associate Archivist for Collections Management at the New York State Archives and Records Administration, Cultural Education Center, Albany, NY 12230.

from local systems to cooperative regional and national networks. The involvement of archives in automation, primarily during the past decade, has raised the issue of integrating archival and manuscripts records into library systems, and how those systems can be used to support archival functions.

Besides economic concerns, the variant approaches to library and archives practice pose potential constraints on shared systems as well. Historically libraries and archives have debated their relationship, with archivists and librarians commonly emphasizing the differences in both their materials and techniques. Even among those institutions having a library and an archives, separate catalogs and reference facilities have been common. With automation's onset, the archival profession has experienced a rapid turnabout. Following close on the adoption of the MARC Format for Archives and Manuscripts Control, archivists have shown considerable interest in library cataloging, indexing practices, and related standards. For political, economic, and technical reasons, many archivists and manuscript librarians have begun using library systems such as RLIN, OCLC, GEAC, VTLS, and NOTIS to automate control of and access to their holdings.

After operating several years within library automated systems, archivists have found themselves to be in neither a totally foreign land, nor a comfortable home. A variety of common library system design characteristics needs to be analyzed in relationship to archival materials and archival practices. Only when a careful assessment has taken place can archivists determine whether a given library system can adequately provide management of and access to archival and manuscript holdings. That analysis can also serve as a tool for determining whether or what changes to the system can be instituted to provide additional control of and access to archival materials.

A range of factors need to be analyzed. The differences in the nature of library and archival materials is a consideration in such an assessment, since they have significant impact on the functions performed by libraries and archives. Bibliographic description and information retrieval are the most obviously similar functions, yet specific differences and issues regarding these need to be addressed. Some of the features needed for archives may provide new dimensions that would be useful to librarians if developed. Some archival operations might not be provided for in library systems, at which point serious consideration must be given to alternate means for accomplishing those functions. Ultimately, archivists and librarians will have to determine whether sufficient political, technical, and economic factors exist to make the use of shared automated systems viable.

DIFFERENCES IN THE NATURE
OF ARCHIVAL AND LIBRARY MATERIALS

Before delineating the differences between archival and library materials, it is useful to focus on why archivists and librarians would consider shared systems. The simple but essential fact is that both are valuable sources of information. In contemporary society, dubbed "The Information Age," there is a tremendous need for a wide range of data. The source, whether a library or archives, is far less important than the information itself. As a result, library and archives users are often very similar, and a user seeking information might need both archival and library materials. This need to provide information to users results in a number of functions that are very similar, at least at the most general level. The USMARC Formats for Bibliographic Data (UFBD) is clear evidence of the commonalities in library and archival information.

Some core differences need to be kept in mind, however. Particularly significant is the intent with which library and archival materials are created. Library materials are the conscious product of the work of an author or authors. A book on Great Lakes pollution is the intended result of a research and writing process. It is meant to be comprehensible as a unit. As a result, library materials are autonomous. That is, they can be read or viewed, and understood on their own without having supporting explanations, background, or additional information. Archival and manuscript materials are much different in intent. They are the by-products of human activity, the traces of documents, photographs, maps, or other forms of material left by a group or individual. They are the means to an end, not the end in themselves. A public interest group might generate a range of correspondence, reports, statistical data, and other information relating to water pollution in the Great Lakes. Those files cannot be read through and result in a coherent picture of Great Lakes water pollution. Archival and manuscript materials cannot adequately be understood on their own; interpretive and background information is needed to provide the context. This has significant impact on describing, retrieving, and managing archival materials.

Library materials are described and controlled generally at the item level. As a result, library standards provide rules for cataloging based on various forms of material—books, serials, maps, music, and so forth. Archival materials are described and controlled generally as groups. John Steinbeck's personal correspondence is treated as an aggregate; each letter is not treated as a separate entity. As a result, archival and manuscript collections or series can consist of one form of material, or a mixture such as papers, photographs, and maps.

Finally, library materials are generally mass-produced. There are thousands of copies, as well as many editions, of Steinbeck's *The Grapes of Wrath*. A collection of Steinbeck's personal correspondence, however, contains unique, one-of-a kind items. While those might be microfilmed, transcribed, or excerpted, that grouping of original letters is a unique entity, with special descriptive, retrieval, preservation, and security problems.

As noted previously, despite their differences, libraries and archives both serve as information sources for the user public. The variance in intent of creation, the need for context to understand archival records, and the item versus aggregate approach are important factors. They have considerable impact on system design and on the final viability of a shared library and archives system.

LIBRARY AND ARCHIVES FUNCTIONS

Librarians and archivists are able to share a common communications format, the USMARC Format for Bibliographic Data, despite the differences in library and archival materials. That ability to share the MARC Format has been instrumental in leading many archives to consider and to become involved in using library systems. Once again, information is the common ground. As use of the MARC format shows, whether books, serials, maps and so forth, or archives and manuscripts, the information collected by libraries and archives about their holdings has many similarities. Differences begin to arise more clearly when considering the library and archives in order to acquire, describe, preserve, retrieve, and manage those holdings. These functions have considerable impact on the system's design.

The core library and archival functions can be summarized and compared in Table 1. Other non-core functions exist, but are more likely to depend on institutional size and mission.[1]

Most current integrated library systems provide three elements to meet library needs: an acquisitions module covering the acquisition function; a bibliographic module covering the cataloging and retrieval functions; and a circulation module for the circulation function. The management function is commonly provided for by varied types of report production in each module. The differences between library and archival functions become most evident at the point when an archives attempts to adjust its operation to automated library systems. The acquisitions and circulation modules designed for library systems are sufficiently unique that archivists have made no efforts to employ these with their holdings. Archival efforts have relied solely on using library bibliographic modules for archival automation. The remaining discussion will focus primarily on the efforts by archivists to use library bibliographic systems to provide for the description and retrieval functions.

ARCHIVAL USE OF LIBRARY BIBLIOGRAPHIC AND RETRIEVAL SYSTEMS

The archival use of library systems raises a range of issues and problems relating to system design. The aforementioned differences between library and archival materials have impact on both the nature of archival bibliographic records and the process of creating them. Consequently, retrieval of archival bibliographic records also differs. Since the MARC family includes formats for authorities, holdings/location and bibliographic data, the relationship of these formats to archival functions raises additional considerations in system design. The issues and concerns raised here are intended to be

TABLE 1: COMPARISON OF CORE FUNCTIONS

LIBRARY FUNCTIONS

Acquiring holdings: identifying materials needed by the user public; ordering, receiving, and paying for those items.

Cataloging holdings: providing item level control over items in order to facilitate their retrieval by creating a catalog record. retrieving holdings: locating relevant known items for users

ARCHIVAL FUNCTIONS

Appraising potential holdings: assessing materials to determine the value of records, and deciding whether they should be permanently retained or whether they can be destroyed.

Acquiring holdings: transferring custody and ownership of the materials to the repository; establishing initial physical and intellectual control.

Describing holdings: arranging, providing intellectual and physical descriptions, and developing finding aids, which may include a catalog record.

Preserving holdings: taking actions to physically stabilize or protect the physical condition of materials.

Retrieving holdings: identifying and locating holdings that may have useful information for users.

managing holdings: maintaining and manipulating information about materials over their life cycle (e.g. appraisal decisions, source of acquisition, preservation treatments applied, users of the records for security purposes).

Circulating holdings: checking items in and out, putting them on reserve, and conducting inter-library loans.

Managing holdings: preserving brittle or physically endangered items, compiling circulation and use statistics.

illustrative; a comprehensive analysis would be prohibitively long for inclusion in this paper.[2]

Bibliographic Records

The archival bibliographic record as a whole has unique characteristics that are of concern in system design. The dynamic, complex nature of an archival bibliographic record is particularly significant. Library materials are cataloged once; the author will not change over time, for example, nor will the contents, or year and place of publication. If a work is revised or reissued, it will receive a separate, new catalog record. The primary library exception to this is serials, where changes and additions to the bibliographic record may occur. The result of most library cataloging, however, is generally a stable bibliographic record. Archival bibliographic records are dynamic, and often subject to alteration or expansion. The main entry for records received from an insurance company, for example, might change over time as the company reorganizes or merges with another company. Especially if the company is regularly transferring its archival records to a repository as they become inactive, the main entry might change each time new records come to the archives.[3]

Other actions can also affect the stability of the archival record. Donors might contribute some of their papers to an archives or manuscripts repository during their lifetime, at which point an initial archival bibliographic record is created. After their death, a spouse or family member might contribute additional parts of the original donor's papers, which requires the original bibliographic record to be amended to include changes in dates, content, volume, and so forth. In addition, changes made to the original papers given to the archives might take place in the process of describing and preserving the papers. Non-archival materials might be weeded out, or disorganized records arranged for better access. Records might need preservation treatment so indications of actions taken need to be noted. These actions taken by archival staff have some impact on the physical and intellectual nature of the papers, and that information needs to be recorded as well. Most library bibliographic and retrieval systems have not been designed intentionally to facilitate easy changes to records, especially the types of changes needed by archival records. For most systems, inserting a field is possible. However, few have the easy editing features common to word processing, such as block moves or deletions. Some require an entire field to be deleted and re-entered if changes are going to be made. Particularly in narrative note fields, inserting or editing text is often difficult.

The unique nature of archival materials also poses some special problems. For library materials, copy-cataloging is a significant means for producing bibliographic records. With archival materials, this is not possible, so all bibliographic records require original cataloging. Library systems are not always designed to ensure the ease of this process. A useful feature for archives is the establishment of default values for records being entered. For example, in many government archives as well as organizational archives, the main entry for most holdings will begin with a consistent name such as New York (State), AFL-CIO, Yale University, and so forth. Often a group of records being entered at the same time will also share common subject headings, citation notes, or restriction notes. Entry efficiencies can be greatly facilitated by the ability to establish default values on selected fields.

Because archival bibliographic records describe aggregate groups, they are generally much longer and more complicated than library bibliographic records. Archival bibliographic records have a significant number of note fields, indexing fields, and other information fields. Many of these, such as the biographical/historical note (MARC field 545) and scope/content note (MARC Field 520) are essential components for providing contextual and summary information on the holdings. Archival materials also require a substantial number of indexing fields, particularly names, topical subjects, geographical locations, forms of material, function, and occupations in order to make the information accessible.[4] As a result, systems limiting record or field length can pose serious problems for archival description and cataloging. Some archivists using library systems with limitations on record length have found themselves in the uncomfortable position of artificially breaking up collections in order to enter them online. In other cases, a narrative field such as the scope and content note has to be broken into several repetitions of the MARC 520 field in order to circumvent field length restrictions. The extent of this information can also be problematic for screen displays, since most library systems assume bibliographic records will consist of one or two screens. As a result, many are not designed to accommodate easy movement from first screen to last screen, or back and forth between screens. This can make reviewing archival bibliographic records particularly tiresome, especially if they are part of the results retrieved in a combined format catalog.

System design raises issues not only in creating archival bibliographic records, but also in the retrieval of those records. Again, the differing nature of library and archival materials has impact on the nature of the indexing process. Library materials are much more focussed because they are created to address a definable topic, therefore library indexing is predicated on providing the most specific characterization of the item in hand and the work it contains. Archival materials do not, as previously noted, have a clear focus and as a result pose special problems for indexing. Archival materials will often cover a range of subjects, making more extensive indexing necessary. Those indexing problems then translate into retrieval needs that need to be accommodated in systems, but often are not.

Perhaps the major retrieval concern is the way in which a system treats the currently separate USMARC Formats for Bibliographic Data. Current systems generally take one of two approaches to file structure. The first approach is to enter each format into a separate file, and a user must search each individually. So if a user wishes to see information on grape-workers in California, whether in books, visual materials, or archival and manuscripts holdings, each file must be searched separately. The second approach is to treat all formats as a single file, so searches will retrieve materials on that topic regardless of format. In such systems, a user interested in only one type of material will have to select out materials in their preferred format. Depending on the user public, one of these might be a preferable retrieval mode, but a system where users could choose to search the whole database or to limit it to a certain format would be most preferable.

Retrieval

One area in which specific archival concerns are evident is the retrieval of personal and corporate names. The library concept of "authorship" is generally a clean distinction — authorship is attributed to the person or organization having primary responsibility for creating the cataloged item, and is usually presented on the title page. Archival materials are more appropriately described using the concept of "main entry" based on provenance or creation, rather than authorship. The main entry is attributed to the person or organization having primary responsibility for bringing together or maintaining the collection or series of records. This does not necessarily imply "authorship," that is, having written all the documents. The main entry for a group of letters received by a woman over her life time is the woman herself, although she did not "author" any of the letters she received. She did receive, collect, and maintain those letters, hence she serves as the main entry, the focal point to which the letters relate.

The personal and corporate name issue is further complicated by the distinction made by libraries between names as added entries and names as subjects (the MARC 600/610 and 700/710 fields). Considerable discussion has been underway in the archival community about how to address this distinction. Because of the nature of archival material, many archivists feel a collection of letters received and maintained by Elaine Steinbeck, which includes letters written by John Steinbeck, also reflects significant information about him, hence he might be considered both as an added entry and a subject entry.

Some library systems provide retrieval on personal and corporate names regardless of whether the name is a main, added, or subject entry. Others do segregated searching for names as authors and names as subjects. The way in which the system searches names will have impact on the construction of an archival bibliographic record. Some archivists enter names in the main or added entry fields, then re-enter them in the subject name field in order to assure user retrieval. Others have relied on searching instructions to inform users to search for names in both ways. While either approach might serve as a solution for one particular system, it is problematic when bibliographic records are created in response to a particular system's peculiarities. Difficulties may occur if archival bibliographic records are transferred to another system with a different approach to name searching. This is increasingly common as regional or topical databases are developed, and is particularly evident when archivists attempt to use the two major bibliographic utilities, RLIN and OCLC in combination with a local library system.

Another area where differences in library and archival practice pose problems for retrieval relates to titles. Library titles are generally direct transcriptions from the title page, and might or might not provide the user with a sense of the described item's contents. Archival materials have no assigned titles, but are descriptive titles supplied by the archivist. Those titles are information-rich, and are intended to summarize the holdings described. Library searchers often use a known title as a specific route of access, so systems employing search key type of file access are a quick means for retrieval. It is highly unlikely that archives users will know the supplied title unless they rely on a citation in a published work. Those library systems providing title word retrieval are much more amenable for archival use. It is also useful when Boolean searching can be conducted with title word as one option in the combination.

Subject searching also raises retrieval issues. This is in part a system design issue, but also one of archival practice. Archivists have not articulated any common conceptual framework for indexing methodology, nor have they sufficiently studied users to understand what retrieval methods would be most preferable.[5] This makes a cogent discussion of retrieval needs rather difficult. Some very general needs can be defined, however, as they relate to current system design for subject retrieval. First, there are several distinct types of indexing terms currently available to archivists in the US-MARC AMC Format. While not available in other formats at present, they will become so with format integration. In addition to the standard library index terms, archivists can provide terms for form of material, occupation, and function. Many systems do not presently provide direct access to these terms at all — some allow separate searches. Other systems simply include these fields in the general subject index. While that at least does make the terms accessible, it results in unnecessarily large results. For example, a user who wants to see all holdings containing maps in such a retrieval system would get not only all holdings containing maps, but all those relating to maps as a subject, which might not include any maps at all. This is especially problematic if the system searches all the MARC formats together, because books, serials, and other media about mapping will be retrieved.

Another type of searching useful for archival materials is a search for linked records. Archival materials have complex linkages that are not easily represented through retrieval mechanisms in most library systems. Currently, only one linking field is available for archival materials, the 773 Host/Item linking field. With format integration, a whole range of linking fields will become available to archivists and will receive considerable use to express a variety of complex relationships between records. These include links showing predecessor and successor record relationships, and part-whole relationships. Most systems do not retrieve using these linking fields, but their ability to do so would be highly advantageous to archivists, and might also be useful for librarians.

On the whole, the problems of archival retrieval call for increased sophistication in system retrieval. Most systems provide a limited number of search types, commonly relying on author, title, subject, call number and occasionally others. Within those types there is usually some amount of Boolean searching, and combining of search types, such as author and subject. Many common library searches are usable, but not highly effective for archival searching. Only a very few systems allow the institution itself to define search groups, thereby tailoring retrieval to the repository's materials and users. As a result, archivists and manuscripts librarians are forced to devise intricate search strategies to use library systems.

Archival Uses of Authority Files

To support the creation of bibliographic records, some library systems include authority files, generally the Library of Congress Name Authority File, and the Library of Congress Subject Headings. The primary role of authority files in the library setting has been for headings management, that is, to standardize terminology in order to facilitate information retrieval. Archivists can and do use these authority files also for headings management. The presence of additional indexing fields for archival materials, i.e., form, function, occupation, also require the use of headings management. For these, the Library of Congress Subject Headings are inadequate, so systems would be most adaptable if they provided for authority control using other vocabulary lists and thesauri. Authority control is more useful when it extends beyond simple searching for preferred terms in a separate authority file. As it is certainly also useful for libraries, users of archives should also be directed to the preferred term when entering a non-preferred term during a search. Further, global search and replacement for terms that are changed in the authority file is also a significant feature.

Archivists and manuscripts librarians have additional authority control concerns. David Bearman and Richard Szary have articulated the need for archival authority records.[6] They have suggested an archival authority record to provide significant information about the history and characteristics of people and organizations. This authority record might provide background information on the areas in which the person or organization worked, organizational functions and responsibilities, organizational structure changes, and other information that will help users determine concepts to use in searching. Such an authority record would also serve as a useful source of contextual information helpful in interpreting the archival records related to it. Such authority records would need to be searchable by users along with standard bibliographic information. They would also need the capacity for easy change and updating as new or additional information became available. To date, authority files on library systems have not provided this level of information and flexibility, although it could clearly be useful for library patrons as well.

Holdings/Location Systems

The USMARC Format for Holdings/Location is not currently implemented on many library systems, although with the recent approval of that format, it will begin appearing more frequently. For archivists and manuscript librarians, this might pose some definite problems depending on the system design and implementation. Because archival materials are unique, archives do not have holdings information as libraries do. The only element of the current format relevant to archives, therefore, will be one field, which records the location of the bibliographic entity (MARC field 852). Systems may either embed this field into the bibliographic record, or may choose to create a separate holdings segment, where this information along with other holdings data will reside. Location information embedded in the bibliographic record will not pose major problems for archival users. However, if a separate holdings segment is created, archival users will be required to change from the bibliographic record to the holdings/location record just to obtain one small, but vital piece of information. To archivists and manuscript librarians, this seems an unnecessary and circuitous exercise for users.

ADDRESSING THE CONCERNS AND ISSUES RAISED

As the preceding discussion illustrates, archivists have many concerns relating to systems design. One might be tempted to conclude that these issues preclude the possibility of effectively using the same system for libraries and archives. Library systems are not designed to provide maximum automated access for archives—but they are also not designed to provide maximum automated access for libraries. As noted early in this article, the economic attractions of the library and archives markets are by no means strong to computer system developers. This is evident from the fact that many library systems are developed by companies who deal with libraries as their sole market—they have grown up in response to that need, and many began as library consortiums (such as RLG, OCLC, WLN) or as systems designed for a particular library then generalized to the larger market (such as NOTIS and VTLS). They are often the product of librarians who became involved in systems development and automation, not automation companies who recognized a market and built software for it. Few library automation vendors have the financial capacity for significant research and development efforts in order to design new and ever more sophisticated means of automated cataloging and retrieval. Archives, an even smaller market than libraries, can certainly not expect to develop technologically advanced systems for themselves alone. The economic realities of library and archival automation place very real constraints on the possibilities for system design and development. That must be accepted as a basic premise when automating any library or archives.

Archives and libraries both might benefit from a dialogue regarding functional needs and systems design. Library practice has been instrumental in assisting archivists along the route to automating their holdings. Libraries have traditionally operated with more standardized practices than the eclectic approach evident in archives. Tools such as the *Anglo-American Cataloging Rules*, the *Library of Congress Subject Headings*, and the *USMARC Formats* have proved invaluable as guides for archivists as they have sought to standardize their practices over the past few years. Archivists have learned much about their own needs, and have begun to more clearly articulate their practices in relationship to libraries after experience using automated library systems. Conversely, the different approach that archivists and manuscript librarians take to their material can suggest alternatives to the library community. Library systems traditionally have been oriented toward print materials, with heaviest emphasis on the cataloging and retrieval needs of books. As a result, other kinds of materials in libraries such as serials, microforms, audio-visual materials and maps, have been pressed to conform to somewhat oblique practices. Archival needs are at times only a more extreme form of needs shared by these other library materials. Designing systems to focus on capturing and retrieving *information* as opposed to physical forms of material is a clear and compelling need.

In order for shared systems to be more effective, archivists and librarians need to have a better idea of each other's functions and automated applications. Many librarians are as baffled by archival bibliographic records and the processes that go into creating them as archivists are by the *Anglo-American Cataloging Rules* and some of the MARC Formats. It is impossible to clearly determine the actual points of similarity and difference until librarians and archivists alike step outside their professional parochialities of jargon, historical habits of practice, and the normal human tendency to wish to continue things "as they are." The potential for shared automated systems needs to be assessed in an analytical, conceptual framework if it is to be effective and accurate.

Archivists need to consider what role a shared library and archives system can fill in their overall automation needs. Some archivists had hoped for fully integrated systems allowing the automation of all archival functions. While that is the ultimate goal, as it has been for many libraries, it is unlikely with currently available systems. As a result, archivists must analyze their information needs and put together a rational grouping of automated and manual systems. It is crucial that this information structure not require such significant adaptations of archival practice that future systems be endangered or affected adversely by the systems designed. It will take considerable skill to navigate the course between hopes for the automated future and the pressures of automated expediencies in the present.

The automation odyssey will no doubt strike many as a seemingly endless series of challenges with no assurances of unqualified success. Substantial and significant progress can in fact be made with careful analysis and creative approaches to meeting both temporary and long range goals. Automation is not a task simply to be begun and completed; it will be a constant, ongoing process. While no ideal land will ultimately be reached, the journey can produce improved practice for both librarians and archivists as well as improved access for the users of information in our society.

NOTES

1. More information on archival functions can be found in: H. Thomas Hickerson, "Standards for Archival Information Management Systems," in *American Archivist*, 1990 (forthcoming) and the "Data Elements Dictionary" in Nancy Sahli, *MARC for Archives and Manuscripts: The AMC Format*, Chicago: Society of American Archivists, 1985.

2. For a detailed consideration of functional requirements for archival systems, see David Bearman, *Functional Requirements for Collections Management Systems: Archival Informatics Technical Report*, Pittsburgh: Archives and Museum Informatics, Fall 1987.

3. A description of standard archival practice in determining main entry, as well as other cataloging issues, is in Steven L. Hensen, *Archives, Personal Papers, and Manuscripts*, Chicago: Society of American Archivists, 1989.

4. Form of material and function are not common access points with library materials, but have definite uses with archives and manuscripts. Many archival researchers, for example, are interested in locating specific forms of materials such as diaries, maps, photographs, land deeds, and so forth. Since archival materials can be any or a mixture of forms, it is useful to be able to identify them separately. Function is an important key to contextual information, since it identifies the sphere of activity in which an organization operated, resulting in the creation of records. For more details on the role of function, see Alden N. Monroe and Kathleen D. Roe, "What's the Purpose? Functional Access to Archival Records" in Patricia Molholt and Toni Petersen, *Extending MARC Beyond the Book: Access to Non-traditional Materials*, New York: G.K. Hall, 1990 (forthcoming).

5. Archivists have begun recently to discuss the problems of subject analysis and also user studies. See Avra Michaelson, "Description and Reference in the Age of Automation," *American Archivist*, Spring 1987: 192-208, and Lawrence Dowler, "The Role of Use in Defining Practice and Principles: A Research Agenda for the Availability and Use of Records," *American Archivist*, Winter/Spring 1988: 74-86.

6. See Richard Szary, "Expanding the Role of Authority Files in the Archival Context." Paper presented at the Society of American Archivists Annual Meeting, November 1985, and David Bearman and Richard Szary, "Beyond Authorized Headings: Authorities as Reference Files in a Multi-Disciplinary Setting" in *Authority Control Symposium: Occasional Papers No. 6*, 69-78. Papers presented during the 14th Annual ARLIS/NA Conference, New York, N.Y. February 10, 1986, edited by Karen Muller. Tucson: Art Libraries of North America, 1987.

So That Others May See:
Tools for Cataloging Still Images

Barbara Orbach

SUMMARY. How can we communicate the essence of still images such as photographs in ways that enable potential users to discover the material and to decide whether it meets their needs? This paper examines six critical features of photographs that should be reflected in cataloging, making some comparisons between the cataloging of textual archival and manuscript materials and the cataloging of visual materials. It discusses the role of the catalog record in the work of the repository, and goes on to describe tools recently developed for describing and indexing historical or original visual materials.

We all recognize and, at some level, "read" images when we see them, adjusting to and benefiting from the unique ways in which they communicate. But how can we convey the essence of images in a way that enables potential users to discover the material and to decide whether it meets their needs? How do qualities of pictorial media affect cataloging? Acknowledging the truth of the aphorism "A picture is worth a thousand words," what can we hope to accomplish in creating catalog records—word descriptions—for visual materials? This paper will address some of these questions, making some comparisons between the cataloging of archival and manuscript materials and the cataloging of historical or original visual materials, but concentrating on describing tools that have been developed specially for cataloging the latter materials.

To simplify matters, the focus will be on characteristics of photo-

Barbara Orbach is Cataloger of Pictorial Collections in the Prints and Photographs Division, Library of Congress, Washington, DC 20540.

This paper was adapted from a version presented at the Mid-Atlantic Regional Archives Conference, Williamsburg, Virginia, November 5, 1988.

graphs, but much of what is covered also applies to other types of visual material. In some ways images, as a class of material, are no different from other materials found in libraries, archives, or manuscript collections. In other ways, they pose special challenges.

SIX CRITICAL FEATURES

First of all, photos are not self-identifying. It is usually possible to discern what a photograph is of: a group of Girl Scouts, a fist fight, a bordello. With more effort, one can usually identify the specific persons or places depicted. But generally it is not possible to determine confidently from the visual data presented what the photographer's purpose was in making the image or the circumstances under which it was made.

Of course, photographs may be accompanied by captions or other textual information. Captions like those Lewis Hine wrote as he took photos of child labor conditions almost stand on their own in documenting a situation and a point of view (Figure 1). In fact, photos are, paradoxically, an often overlooked source of textual evidence. At any rate, when used with the same cautions that are applied in evaluating other types of evidence, the text that accompanies images can be vital to the researcher in interpreting the image content and significance. Therefore, it is important to mention in the catalog record the presence of captions and to give some idea of their extent.

This is not to lessen the value of the visual evidence photos contain. Photographs document physical and spacial qualities; they can convey a mood or the sheer visual impact of a situation in a way that few other types of documents can. As in manuscript cataloging, objective summaries that, at the same time, weigh the information value of visual material can be quite useful to the researcher. Likewise, as with manuscripts, the information value of images is often cumulative. More images related to a subject or event mean a more rounded picture. Examining a sequence of action portrayed in photos or comparing the evidence supplied by discrete images can be an important part of visual research. In certain cases, organizing and cataloging images in groups facilitates this type of research.

Like other archival materials, photographs might be a byproduct

FIGURE 1. "Accident to young cotton mill worker. Giles Edmund Newsom (Photo October 23rd, 1912) while working in Sanders Spinning Mill, Bessemer City, N.C., August 21st, 1912 a piece of the machine fell on to his foot mashing his toe. This caused him to fall on to a spinning machine and his hand went into the unprotected gearing, crushing and tearing out two fingers. He told the Attorney he was 11 years old when it happened. His parents are now trying to make him 13 years old. The school census taken at the time of the accident makes him 12 years (parents' statement), and the school record says the same. His brother (see photo 3071) is not yet 11 years old. Both of the boys worked in the mill several months before the accident. His father (R. L. Newsom) tried to compromise with the Company when he found the *boy* would receive the money and not the parents. The mother tried to blame the boys for getting the jobs on their own hook, but she let them work several months. The aunt said 'Now he's a jes got to where he could be of some help to his Ma an' then this happens and he can't never work no more like he oughter.'" Lewis Hine photo for the National Child Labor Committee, Library of Congress Prints and Photographs Division, LOT 7479-5, no. 3073, LC-USZ62-20093.

of the activities of an organization or person. But they are always produced by a conscious impulse to record or express something. The person doing the recording or expressing might or might not be identified; nevertheless, his or her individual vision or artistic and technical aptitude might well be embodied in the image. As more makers of images are identified, researchers are becoming more sophisticated about using information about creators as a filter for their interpretations of the content and meaning of the images. So whenever possible, it is important for the cataloger to pass on whatever information is available about the creators of the images and the circumstances of creation.

Researchers are increasingly recognizing that to make a well founded interpretation of an image, they must also take into account the processes by which it was created and the way in which the visual information is presented. The fact that a solemn looking four-year-old had to hold still for several minutes to have his image recorded on a wet glass plate may explain why he looks so solemn. So exemplars of various photo materials and techniques – the daguerreotype or the panoramic photograph for example – have become the subject of study. Similarly, the intended use or packaging can affect interpretation. The impact of a rather gruesome photo of a lynching was increased ten-fold for one recent researcher using our NAACP photographs, when he turned it over and realized it was intended to be used as a postcard (see Figure 2). Presentation formats – cabinet card, cased photo, photo album – and particular genre, such as portraits, landscape views, and aerial views, are sought for the different types of visual information and meaning they will lend, just as in the textual realm diaries or wills are sought by researchers for their anticipated intellectual content. So it becomes incumbent upon the cataloger to enable that type of access.

Finally, inherent in most photographic processes is the potential for a single image to be reproduced in multiple copies. Photographs are not necessarily unique. Researchers have already discovered that the same image or set of images might exist in several repositories; custodians of the images are only now, with the sharing of information about photo collections, beginning to realize the extent to which this is true. The particular grouping or arrangement of images in each repository is usually unique, but the photos in the

FIGURE 2. Photographic postcard showing preparations for a lynching. NAACP Collection. Library of Congress Prints and Photographs Division, LOT 10647-13, LC-USZ62-35741.

collections often are not. By including the same types of information in our catalog records, stating the arrangement and pertinent access policies, and also mentioning what we take to be distinctive features, we give the researcher a better basis for deciding which images to pursue, and we give ourselves a better chance of discovering enough about each others' holdings to make sensible acquisition, cataloging, and preservation decisions.

To summarize, there are six important features of visual materials to take account of in cataloging: captions; impact; cumulative information value; the significance of creators; physical processes and presentation formats; and the fact that most photos can exist in multiple copies.

FUNCTIONS OF THE CATALOG RECORD

Up to now, this discussion has suggested that the role of the catalog record is mostly to serve the researcher. But what a catalog record should include also depends on what the catalog record is meant to do and the other documentation with which it is intended to work. My assumption is that catalog records are intended to help maintain control over a repository's holdings as well as to inform researchers. I also assume that the catalog record need not stand alone as a finding device: it can work in conjunction with comprehensive repository guides and detailed finding aids to specific collections. My ideal catalog record serves as a point of contact that succinctly provides sufficient description to enable the potential user to decide whether to pursue the matter by examining more extensive finding aids or the material itself. It also keeps the staff informed about the shape and scope of the holdings. Given these assumptions, there are four principal missions any catalog record — be it in a manual file or in an online database — should accomplish.

We've already considered the first two: the record should describe the subjects covered by the image or images, giving some sense of the time period of coverage; it should also identify, if possible, organizations or persons involved in making the photographs, since the subjective or artistic elements the makers impart may bear on the content of the images. The description serves a third mission by indicating how many images are involved: is it a single photo or a group of thousands? Are all the images distinct or do some carry the same image content in different forms—negatives and corresponding photoprints, for example? At its most refined, the record indicates what photo processes and presentation formats are involved, with an indication of quantities of each.

Numbers are important not only for the repository's control functions, but also as an indication to the user of how much effort will be required to use the material. This relates to the fourth mission of the catalog record, to which we have also alluded: suggesting to the potential user how much effort will be required to comprehend and extract data from the materials and informing him or her of supplementary aids. If the photos are grouped, how are they organized? Is there identifying information available on or with the photos? In published or unpublished finding aids? In other published sources? How will the repository's access or reproduction policies affect ease of use? Are surrogates or reproductions of the images available, for instance in microform or in published sources? Is there closely related photographic, manuscript, or other material to which the researcher should be alerted?

These elements of information are, in fact, no different than the kinds of information one would supply about any research material. The general approach is certainly—indeed, intentionally—the same; but how much is described in a single record and what is emphasized depends on qualities of the material, as well as institutional appraisal and service policies. As in the description of other types of research material, cataloging decisions are shaped by determinations made earlier. Appraisal of the material determines what will be kept and feeds into arrangement decisions. Is there any original order worth preserving? Are photographs and associated textual material so integrally related that they must remain together? If so, photos will remain interspersed with the textual materials. Leaving aside the preservation consequences of this approach, the cataloging consequence is probably that, if the photos are deemed of sufficient merit, they will receive some mention in the collection description. This approach can be seen, for instance, in *National Union Catalog of Manuscript Collections* (*NUCMC*) entries, where photos within some collections are given sufficiently specific mention to enable the *NUCMC* cataloger to provide an entry for the photographs in the *NUCMC* index.

In contrast, the photos might form an independent component of the collection, housed in a series of their own. One option would be to catalog the photo series separately, in order to bring out qualities of the visual materials, and then link it to the catalog record for the entire collection. In still other cases, the collection is composed entirely of photographs. It may be a truly archival unit, based on provenance, or it may be a unit formed at the repository based on other features, such as a common creator or subject matter. Finally, it is possible that an image will be treated as a single item, either because it was acquired as such, or, more likely, because it is considered of such value as an object that it merits description and control all on its own.

Obviously, the structure, missions, and resources of the repository will influence arrangement decisions. Once these are made, the limits of the work being described in the catalog record can be defined. Photographs, like manuscripts, can be cataloged as single items, or they can be described as collections or assembled groups. In fact, given time and careful analysis, it is possible to describe photographs at two or more related levels — an item or subgroup and the collection to which it belongs, for instance. (Figures 3-5 illustrate some of the levels of treatment possible.)

CATALOGING TOOLS

Having determined *what* to catalog, it remains to formulate the description in a coherent and concise fashion and to assign consistently the index terms that lead the user to the description. Here, the choice of cataloging tools comes into play. First, there are the tools that guide the cataloger in describing the material. As I have already suggested, certain types of information are routinely needed in the catalog record. Cataloging manuals have been written to ensure that appropriate information is supplied in a consistent fashion. The *Anglo-American Cataloguing Rules*, 2nd edition, 1988 revision (*AACR 2*) provides some guidance in describing visual materials, but it does not come to terms with the full variety of decisions one faces in trying to describe unpublished or historical graphic items or collections. Elisabeth Betz Parker, of the Library of Congress Prints and Photographs Division, compiled the manual *Graphic Materials: Rules for Describing Original Items and Historical Collections*[1] to supplement *AACR 2*. *Graphic Materials* offers solutions for questions like "How do I express dimensions for a group of photographs on original mounts?" or "Where do I put information about attributions?" It doesn't make all the decisions for you; you have to know, for instance, what your institution wishes to count: Negatives *and* corresponding photoprints? Just the negatives? Just the photoprints? In numbers of items or in linear feet? But once those decisions are made, *Graphic Materials* shows patterns for communicating the information effectively.

Steve Hensen's *Archives, Personal Papers, and Manuscripts* (*APPM*) can be used to describe collections that include visual materials. *APPM* was written at the same time as *Graphic Materials*, also as a supplement to *AACR 2*. In fact, in many respects the two supplementary manuals run in parallel. *APPM* does not address, however, the special qualities of visual materials. It does not help resolve situations only encountered with graphic materials, such as where to mention markings on or captions accompanying the images, or how to describe published pictorial works or multi-part works.

Since both manuals offer options at a number of points, leaving much to cataloger judgment, it must be emphasized that the most important tool for cataloging visual materials is the cataloger. What the cataloger chooses to include in the description and the clarity with which that information is expressed determines not only how well those using the record will understand it but whether, in fact, it can be found at all, since the information in the catalog record forms the basis for supplying access points—the names, titles, or headings by which the searcher is led to the record. Consistency in determining what access points should be supplied is crucial because the access points provide the avenues to the descriptions; collectively, access points serve to highlight relationships among records—and the materials they represent.

Access points are used as an avenue to a number of features of visual material: names associated with the creation or collection of the material, as well as subjects, forms, genre, and physical pro-

Figure 3. Sample USMARC record from Library of Congress, Prints and
Photographs Division. Record describing a collection.

001 88-707696 PP

050 Prints and Photographs Division Collection

245 Frances Benjamin Johnston Collection (Library of Congress) [graphic].

260 ca. 1864-ca. 1947, bulk 1897-1927.

300 ca. 25,000 items.

351 Bulk arranged in over 110 groups (lots) based on subject matter and
     cataloged with a (710) added entry of "Frances Benjamin Johnston
     Collection (Library of Congress)." Some material, including Johnston's
     original negatives, has been incorporated into filing series for
     special formats.

520 Primarily photographs by Johnston, including portraits of prominent
     Americans, foreign dignitaries, and members of Washington, D.C., social
     and political circles. Photojournalistic coverage of American politics
     & government, industry, social conditions, and events, ca. 1890-1913.

Architecture in the United States, concentrating on the South,

Mid-Atlantic, New England, and the Pacific Coast, ca. 1913-1940.

Travels in Europe, Middle East, Bermuda, and across the United States,

ca. 1899-1922. Also includes material collected by Johnston, such as

artistic photos by other photographers, family photos, albums, graphic

ephemera, and architectural and watercolor drawings.

545   One of the first women to achieve prominence as a photographer,

Johnston opened a studio in Washington, D.C., in 1890, carrying out

portrait and photojournalism assignments. She entered into partnership

with Mattie Edwards Hewitt, operating a New York City studio that

specialized in architectural and garden photography, 1913-1917.

Continuing this emphasis, Johnston toured the United States giving

lantern slide lectures on gardens and architecture and contributed to

architectural surveys, including two separate collections: the

Pictorial Archives of Early American Architecture (1930) and the

Carnegie Survey of the Architecture of the South (1933-1937).

555   Additional information available in unpublished general finding aid

FIGURE 3 (continued)

filed in P&P Reading Room Reference File.

541   Most are gift and purchase, Frances Benjamin Johnston and Johnston estate, 1905-1953.

541   Some transferred from LC Manuscript Division (Frances Benjamin Johnston Papers), 1982. DLC/PP-1982:211.

541   A few are copyright deposits of Johnston.

510   Special Collections in the Library of Congress / compiled by Annette Melville. Washington, D.C. : Library of Congress, 1980, no. 131.

510   Guide to the Special Collections of Prints and Photographs in the Library of Congress / compiled by Paul Vanderbilt. Washington, D.C. : Library of Congress Reference Department, 1955.

600   Johnston, Frances Benjamin, 1864-1952.

650   Politics & government--1890-1920. [1ctgm]

650   Events--1890-1920. [1ctgm]

650   Industry--United States--1890-1920. [1ctgm]

650   Economic & social conditions--1890-1920. [1ctgm]

650   Architecture—United States—1910-1940. [lctgm]

650   Travel—1890-1930. [lctgm]

650   Families—1860-1950. [lctgm]

651   United States.

655   Portrait photographs—1860-1950. [gmgpc]

700   Johnston, Frances Benjamin, 1864-1952.

700   Johnston, Frances Benjamin, 1864-1952. Papers, 1855-1954.

755   Photographs 1860-1950. gmgpc

040   gihc

043   n-us---

007   khummm

Figure 4. Sample USMARC record from Library of Congress, Prints and
Photographs Division. Record describing subunit of the Frances Benjamin
Johnston Collection

001 87-707145 PP

050 LOT 12643 (G) <P&P>

100 Johnston, Frances Benjamin, 1864-1952, photographer.

245 Virginia architecture and gardens [graphic].

260 ca. 1905-ca. 1933.

300 517 photoprints : 506 silver gelatin, 9 cyanotype, 2 albumen ; 27 x 35
     cm. or smaller.

300 2 photomechanical prints ; 9 x 14 cm.

351 Arranged alphabetically by county, followed by Skyline Drive views and
     unidentified Va. sites.

520 Estates—especially Mount Vernon and Oatlands, dwellings, mills, and a
     few commercial and educational buildings in Virginia towns and rural
     areas. Includes interiors, architectural elements such as ceilings,

stairways, fireplaces, and doors; art works, including portrait paintings. Alexandria streets, with blacks at work and leisure; gardens and garden ornaments, forests, ponds, and roads.

545   Johnston probably took the photos for the Carnegie Survey of Architecture of the South (see LOT 11841 for set of photoprints made by the Library of Congress from Johnston's negatives).

555   List of sites available in Prints and Photographs Reading Room, filed by lot number.

500   Title devised. Most photos captioned; Johnston numbers on some.

500   Includes one photo by Howard C. Cobbs; some possibly by other photographers.

500   Includes photos printed from the same negative by different processes.

500   One hundred and twenty-eight are photos made by the Library of Congress Photoduplication Service from original glass or nitrate negatives in series LC-J7, J70, J698, and J699.

500   Accompanied by brochure on Arlington House.

541   Gift and purchase, Frances Benjamin Johnston estate, 1953?

FIGURE 4 (continued)

541 Some transfers, Manuscript Division (Frances Benjamin Johnston Papers),
     1982. (DLC/PP-1982:211)

500 Forms part of the Frances Benjamin Johnston Collection; for general
     information, see collection record with title: Frances Benjamin
     Johnston Collection (Library of Congress).

500 Related, larger photoprints by Johnston are in LOT 12629.

610 Oatlands (Va.)

650 Educational buildings--Virginia--1900-1940 . [lctgm]

650 Commercial buildings--Virginia--1900-1940. [lctgm]

650 Estates--Virginia--1900-1940. [lctgm]

650 Gardens--Virginia--1900-1940. [lctgm]

650 Dwellings--Virginia--1900-1940. [lctgm]

650 Afro-Americans--Virginia--Alexandria.

650 Architectural elements--Virginia--1900-1940. [lctgm]

650 Interiors--Virginia--1900-1940. [lctgm]

650 Streets--Virginia--1900-1940. [lctgm]

650 Roads--Virginia--1900-1940. [lctgm]

650 Forests--Virginia--1900-1940. [lctgm]

650 Lakes & ponds--Virginia--1900-1940. [lctgm]

650 Mills--Virginia--1900-1940. [lctgm]

650 Portrait paintings--1900-1940. [lctgm]

651 Virginia.

651 Alexandria (Va.)

651 Skyline Drive (Va.)

651 Mount Vernon (Va. : Estate)

655 Postcards--1900-1940. [gmgpc]

655 Portraits--1900-1940. [gmgpc]

FIGURE 4 (continued)

700   Cobbs, Howard C., photographer.

710   Frances Benjamin Johnston Collection (Library of Congress)

755   Silver gelatin photoprints 1900-1940. gmgpc

755   Cyanotypes 1900-1940. gmgpc

755   Albumen photoprints 1900-1940. gmgpc

755   Photomechanical prints 1900-1940. gmgpc

755   Reproductions 1900-1940. gmgpc

040   gihc

043   n-us-va

007   khumo-

007   kfubo-

Figure 5. Sample USMARC record from Library of Congress, Prints and
Photographs Division. Record describing a single item. (Includes full MARC
content designation.)

001      $ ab $87-703030 $ PP

050 00 $ abu $MPH – Cameron, $ no. 6 $ (B size) <P&P>

100 1 $ ade $Cameron, Julia Margaret Pattle, $ 1815-1879, $ photographer.

245 14 $ ahc $The Lord Bishop of Winchester $[graphic] / $from life,
                registered photograph copyright Julia Margaret Cameron,
                Freshwater.

260     $ c $c1871 12 Aug.

300     $abc $1 photoprint :$ albumen ;$ image 36 x 28 cm., on mount 50 x 28
                cm.

5200 $a $Half-length portrait of Samuel Wilberforce.

500     $a5 $Title pencilled on mount. $DLC

500     $a5 $Signed in ink on mount. $DLC

500     $a5 $Colmachi stamp on mount. $DLC

FIGURE 5 (continued)

541    $cade $Exchange, $ Schoelkopf, $ 1973.   DLC/PP-1973:302.

037    $abf $LC-USZ62-97016 $ DLC $ (b&w copy photo)

600 10 $ad $Wilberforce, Samuel, $ 1805-1873.

650 -7 $azzy2$Bishops $ England $ Winchester $ 1870-1880. $1ctgm

655 -7 $ay2 $Portrait photographs $ 1870-1880. $gmgpc

755    $ay2 $Albumen photoprints $ 1870-1880. $gmgpc

040    $e $g1hc

007    $a $khuboo

005    $a $000000000000000.0

(Fixed fields) 01.-   02.nnn   03.k   04.n   05.-   06.----- 07.

   08.   09.   10.-   11.   12.   13.   14.

15.eng   16.   17.   18.   19.   20.s   21.1871

22.----   23.xx   24.   25.   26.   27.m   28.-

29.-   30.y   31.-   32.-   33.7   34.-   35.7

36.a   37.   38.f   39.f   40.   41.k

cesses represented. Every bit as important as the choices about *which* access points to supply are the choices we make about which words to use. Consistency is equally vital in this activity. If we refer to it as the World's Columbian Exposition in describing one group of images and the Chicago World's Fair in describing another, the relationship between the materials will not be readily apparent to the researcher.

There are several means by which we maintain consistency in the words we use as access points. To ensure that we express the proper name of a person, place, or thing in the same way it has been used before in catalog records, we rely on two authority files: the Library of Congress Name Authority File and the *Library of Congress Subject Headings*. If the name is not already there, we do the necessary authority work to add it to those files, which are distributed to other institutions via microfiche, MARC tape subscription, or, recently, via CD-ROM.

Doing authority work involves discerning any conflicts with names already in the files, formulating the name, and supplying appropriate cross references. Obtaining the information necessary to formulate a name can be a challenge when one is dealing with a medium where words are secondary to the visual content, and, therefore, are expressed informally or are not recorded at all on the material. We gather the data needed to make heading decisions from the material itself, but also rely heavily on reference sources; then we filter our findings on a given heading through *AACR 2* guidelines. Since authority work is acknowledged to be the most time-consuming part of cataloging, we hope that the effort we spend on authority work will save the time of the next cataloger who has occasion to use the name in the course of cataloging—or the next searcher who looks for material related to that name.

Proper nouns are a vital part of retrieval in archival repositories. But a good share of picture researchers—at least at the Library of Congress (LC)—come in requesting generic topics. For example, events in the autumn of 1989 stirred interest in images of earthquake damage and Polish naval vessels. And there are ongoing requests for images portraying segregation and race relations.

Some of the same challenges images pose to name authority work also affect the process of subject analysis. Whereas a book cataloger might look at a book's title page, table of contents, text, and illustrations and derive a pretty good sense of its major themes and author's point of view, images commonly lack such textual clues. And while a cataloger of a group of manuscripts might reasonably suppose that the papers or records associated with a person or body relate to the principal interests or functions of that individual or organization, images are not always so directly related to the interests or functions of their creators or collectors. In addition to the intricate array of concrete things images may depict, they may carry many layers of meaning, and their themes sometimes lie in the eyes — and interests — of the beholder. The goal of subject analysis is to capture the essence of an image or group of images — its major content and themes — while remaining on the lookout for elements known to be of special interest to the repository's clientele. While analysis is an intellectual task that precedes the assignment of headings, the structure and content of the tool from which the headings are drawn can be of considerable help.

Headings for topics found in pictures could certainly be constructed using terms from the well-known *Library of Congress Subject Headings (LCSH)*. But many of the terms and conventions used in *LCSH* are not well suited to pictorial materials, and some commonly depicted concepts, like "MOONLIGHT" or "MUSHROOM CLOUDS," are too specific for that general list. Moreover, *LCSH* has been constructed primarily for cataloging textual materials, and the guidance it offers does not always translate well into the realm of visual materials. In an effort to fill these gaps, LC Prints & Photographs Division staff extracted the most appropriate terms from *LCSH*, consulted other sources like the *Art and Architecture Thesaurus (AAT)*, and created a thesaurus that includes a network of terms, scope notes, and relationships most applicable to images in general picture collections. The result is the *LC Thesaurus for Graphic Materials*, which is published by the Library of Congress and is authorized for use in the MARC formats.[2] Its value for indexing picture collections lies not only in the availability of terms for objects and ideas commonly appearing in images, but in the guidance it offers. Say you are gazing dubiously at a box of photos showing members and activities of a local friendly society. Should you call it *Friendly societies*? *LCTGM* says "Use *FRATERNAL*

ORGANIZATIONS," and when you look under that term, you see both a note for researchers (PN or public note) "Includes activities and structures," and a note for the cataloger (CN or cataloger's note) "Double index under ORGANIZATIONS' BUILDINGS for images that focus on buildings" (see Figure 6). This sort of guidance aids catalogers in making consistent indexing decisions when faced with similar images—making it possible for researchers to retrieve the maximum number of relevant images in searching a given term.

As mentioned earlier, researchers are becoming interested in certain forms, genre, and physical processes that affect the way in which subject matter is represented. And, as recall increases with consistency of indexing and the sheer number of images retrievable by topic or creator, researchers use type or genre of material to limit or focus their search results. They ask for posters by Ben Shahn, as opposed to his photographs, or they seek group portraits of Civil War soldiers—not individual portraits or scenes of men engaged in military activity.

To anticipate these needs, we select terms from another thesaurus, *Descriptive Terms for Graphic Materials*.[3] Like the topical terms thesaurus, this is an alphabetical list, this time of genre and physical characteristic terms. It provides scope notes explaining their meaning, shows broader, narrower, and related terms, provides references from non-preferred terms, and even indicates the MARC field in which the term should be entered (Figure 7). Genre terms go in the 655 field of the MARC record and physical characteristics terms in the 755 field. The list is intended to cover a broad range of pictorial types, from *glass photonegatives* to *watercolor drawings*, *architectural elevations* to *formation photographs*. Terms from this list can be used to bring out pictorial elements in *any* form of material, whether a book, a piece of music, or a manuscript collection.

There are other lists of form and genre terms; for instance, the list variably known as the "Cornell" list, the "RLIN" list, or Engst and Hickerson's "Form Terms for Archives and Manuscript Collections," as well as lists prepared by the Association of College and Research Libraries' Rare Book and Manuscript Standards Committee. Genre and physical characteristic terms are found in *LCSH*

Figure 6. Sample entries from LC Thesaurus for Graphic Materials: Topical Terms for Subject Access.

Franchise

    USE Suffrage

Franking privilege

    UF   Penalty mail

    BT   Postal service rates

Fraternal organizations

    --[country or state]--[city]

    PN   Includes activities and structures.

    CN   Double index under ORGANIZATIONS' BUILDINGS for images that focus on buildings.

    UF   Benevolent societies

          Friendly societies

          Masonic organizations

Secret societies

BT Organizations

NT Farmers' groups

    Fraternities & sororities

RT Charitable organizations

    Clubs

    Patriotic societies

Fraternities & sororities

    --[country or state]--[city]

PN For fraternal organizations associated with colleges and universities, including their professional fraternities, honor societies, and social societies. Includes activities and structures.

CN Double index under CLUBHOUSES for images that focus on buildings.

UF College fraternities

    Sororities

BT Fraternal organizations

PN = Public note; CN = Cataloger's note; UF = Used for term

BT = Broader term; NT = Narrower term; RT = Related term

Figure 7. Sample entries from Descriptive Terms for Graphic Materials, which includes genre, form, and physical characteristic headings.

Cyanotypes   [755]

PN   Blue photoprints employing light-sensitive iron salts, most commonly on paper; introduced in the 1840s but not in general use until after 1880; often used as proofs.

BT   Monochromatic works

     Photoprints

NT   Blueprints

RT   Proofs >   [755]

Daguerreotypes   [755]

PN   Direct-image photographs on silver-coated copper; introduced in 1839 and in general use until ca. 1860; distinctive mirror-like surface; commonly in a case.

CN   Used in a note under PHOTOGRAPHS and STEREOGRAPHS.

UF   Cased photographs

BT   Photographs

Dance cards   [655]

    PN   Cards on which names of dances and dance partners may be written.

    BT   Cards

Dealers' marks   [755]

    PN   Marks of dealers, auction houses, or other sellers.

    BT   Marks

Death certificates   [655]

    BT   Certificates

and in *AAT*. In the next few years communities using these various tools will have to work together to settle on which list to use in indexing different media or, alternatively, how to square the overlaps among the lists so that a cataloger choosing the term PHOTO-GRAPHS from the Cornell list will still make his or her record retrievable with records indexed using terms from *Descriptive Terms for Graphic Materials* or other lists.[4]

Looking at these choices from a retrieval point of view in an automated, as opposed to a manual, environment means not only matching words and phrases, but putting these words or phrases in the same, predictable place in the record—which brings us to the MARC format. These days, discussions of cataloging often begin with the MARC format. One point driven home during the Use of MARC Records for Archival Visual Materials conference[5] was that some of the participants' decisions about the *content* of the catalog records were influenced by options posed in the MARC format and how their particular automated systems handled the MARC format. Another realization was that, although the discussion began with the one thing the participants all had in common—their use of the packaging device, the MARC format—they inevitably had to backtrack. They had to gain an understanding of the more crucial, preliminary issues I have just gone over. How do each institution's policies on appraisal, arrangement, and service shape its goals in creating catalog records? How much room do these allow for sharing description conventions such as those outlined in the *Graphic Materials* manual and to match on access points through the use of tools like shared authority files, and thesauri for subject and genre terms? Before we can capitalize on the power the MARC format offers for communicating or automating catalog information, we must ask ourselves and each other what our reasons for creating the catalog records are in the first place.

CONCLUSION

With respect to control and cataloging of photographs, we must first come to a shared understanding of their value as research material and their significant characteristics. This paper began by outlining picture characteristics that are important to researchers. But much is still not known about how people work with pictures, and how more effective work could be done. One way to gain a better understanding is to play researcher ourselves: Think about what research questions photographs in your collections might address. Search for photographs that relate to your popularly requested topics and think about what kinds of information affect your searching decisions. Examine a body of photographs and think about which aspects of the images influence your interpretation of the material.

Much work is currently going into analyzing and developing standards for describing and indexing archival material of all types. Standards for describing visual material will doubtlessly evolve as a result of this effort and in recognition of new insights into the nature of visual material and how it is sought. For in developing standard tools and techniques, we must always keep in sight the twin goals of controlling our collections effectively and, at the same time, helping researchers find what they want to see.

NOTES

1. Elisabeth Betz Parker, comp., *Graphic Materials: Rules for Describing Original Items and Historical Collections* (Washington, D.C.: Library of Congress, 1982).

2. Elisabeth Betz Parker, comp., *LC Thesaurus for Graphic Materials: Topical Terms for Subject Access* (Washington, D.C.: Library of Congress, 1987).

3. Helena Zinkham and Elisabeth Betz Parker, comps. and eds., *Descriptive Terms for Graphic Materials: Genre and Physical Characteristic Headings* (Washington, D.C.: Library of Congress, 1986).

4. For a discussion of the various form, genre, and physical characteristic lists and the issues involved in using them for indexing and retrieval, see Jackie M. Dooley and Helena Zinkham, "The Object as 'Subject': Access to Genres, Forms of Material, and Physical Characteristics," in *Extending MARC Beyond the Book* (G.K. Hall, forthcoming, 1990).

5. Gallaudet University, March 30-April 1, 1988, sponsored by the National Historical Publications and Records Commission. A report of the proceedings is included in Linda J. Evans and Maureen O'Brien Will, *MARC for Archival Visual Materials: A Compendium of Practice* (Chicago: Chicago Historical Society, 1988).

Cataloging Sound Recordings Using Archival Methods

David H. Thomas

SUMMARY. Archival collections are usually considered to comprise primarily printed or written material. This paper discusses processing archival sound recording collections. Sound recordings can be archival. That is, they can be: (a) material gathered to accomplish some activity; and (b) material not created for public consumption. The concept of original order, of prime importance in archival work, is sometimes difficult to reconstruct. However, standard archival methods of arrangement can be followed. With sound recordings, the finding aid is usually the only tool for access to any part of a collection. Subject access to archival sound recordings tends to be through forms rather than topics. Cataloging archival sound recordings collections in many ways is similar to cataloging of textual archival collections.

Archival collections are usually considered to comprise primarily printed or written material — in other words, paper-based collections. This view is commonly held outside of the field, but also persists to some degree within it. That this attitude is perpetuated is understandable; the primary method of documentation of human activity has for millennia been the written word on paper, and it is only logical that repositories be dominated by this type of material. However, beginning in the late nineteenth century and continuing to the present day, mankind has invented newer modes of capturing these human acts — methods that do not use paper, are not constrained by the limitations that writing on paper imposes, and which

David H. Thomas is Sound Recording Archivist/Cataloger at the Rodgers & Hammerstein Archives of Recorded Sound, The New York Public Library at Lincoln Center, 111 Amsterdam Avenue, New York, NY 10023.

have thus evolved into different sources of information storing different forms of data. These different forms of capturing information can still be archival, but their content requires that they must be treated differently from more "traditional" archival formats. This paper will discuss some of these differences, and offer some solutions that have been used at the Rodgers & Hammerstein Archives of Recorded Sound (R & H) to process archival sound recording collections.

That so-called "other format" material can even be called archival is still itself somewhat debated. *Archives, Personal Papers and Manuscripts* (*APPM*) summarizes the "print-only" attitude when it states that ". . . such non-textual materials as graphics (including photographs), machine-readable files, and motion pictures and videorecordings may be cataloged according to other rules."[1] Although every archivist likes to call attention to the apocryphal "shoe collection" present in his or her repository, many archivists, when presented with a collection of material that consists primarily of audio or visual material, feel that this material would better belong in a library that is dedicated to the type of material in question, and cataloged using the appropriate MARC format. Presumably, archivists have done this largely because they believe that specialized libraries can better describe and administer these other media.

The belief that libraries can process sound recordings more efficiently is for the most part true, and results from the fact that libraries have a longer history of processing audiovisual materials, and thus that librarians have established policies on how to process them. However, while detailed rules and manuals exist for library sound recording cataloging, cataloging sound recordings as archival entities requires a blending of archival and sound recordings cataloging practices.

But these practices are fundamentally opposed. The tradition in sound recordings cataloging is to break up the contents of each physical item on an intellectual basis to provide access to each work on the item. This conflicts with archival tradition, which usually seeks to unite intellectual entities made up of many physical fragments. For example, although finding aids often include detailed information about larger groupings, more frequently a large group of items will be gathered together as a unit — for example, "Correspondence.'' To respect the traditions of both fields, the sound recordings archivist must devise a hybrid method that will respect both traditions simultaneously.

DEFINING ARCHIVAL SOUND RECORDINGS

Archivists first define archival material as material that is gathered by some person or organization to accomplish some activity, or material that documents the activities of some person or organization.[2] By that definition, sound recordings can be archival; for example, a collection of recordings collected by a conductor of all the rehearsals and performances of a certain orchestra might be considered archival. Second, archival material is usually not created for public consumption, as most books or commercial recordings are, but comes into existence as an outgrowth of some activity of a group or individual, and thus for the most part is unique and unpublished. Sound recordings, like print materials, break down into these two broad categories. Just as archivists tend to treat collections of unpublished materials archivally, a collection of recordings that are all unpublished, or noncommercial, might be treated archivally. Finally, archival collections derive additional importance from context, or the relation of one item to another, both internally and relative to other collections. Collections of sound recordings often fulfill all of these criteria.

An example of a collection of sound recordings that has been treated archivally and cataloged using the Archival and Manuscripts Control (AMC) MARC format at R & H is the Lawrence and Lee collection of noncommercial sound recordings (see Figure 1). These recordings were donated by Jerome Lawrence and Robert Lee, an important creative team that has been active in radio and musical theater since the 1930's. The recordings in the collection document their activities from early in their career into the 1970's, and include not only recordings of performances, but also lectures, interviews, and creative consultations for shows they were writing. These recordings fulfill the main archival criteria: they have a provenance, they are noncommercial, and they gain contextual value when considered as documentation of the Lawrence and Lee collab-

Figure 1: AMC record for a sound recordings collection treated archivally:

ID: NYPW88-A22 RTYP:d ST:s MS: EL: AD:09/24/87
CC: nyu BLT:bc DCF:a CSC:d MOD: PROC:p UD:04/12/88
PP:nyu L:eng PC:i PD:1942/1966 REP:?
MMD: OR: POL: DM: RR: COL: EML: GEN: BSE:
040 NN $c NN $e appm
100 10 Lawrence, Jerome, $d 1915-
245 00 Lawrence and Lee collection of broadcast recordings $h [sound recording], $f 1942-1966.
300 747 sound discs + 94 sound tapes :$b analog.
300 $3 747 sound discs : $b analog, 33 1/3 rpm ; $c 16 in.
300 $3 1 sound tape : $b analog, mono., 15 ips ; $c 10 in.
300 $3 46 sound tapes : $b analog ; $c 7 in.
300 $3 5 sound tapes : $b analog ; $c 5 in.
351 I. Armed Forces Radio Service shows. II. Shows cataloged separately. III. Individual programs. IV. Speeches and appearances. V. Interviews. VI. Production notes, demos and reviews.

545   Jerome Lawrence and Robert Lee are a creative team who have
written, adapted, and produced scripts for radio broadcasts,
television programs, and musical theatre productions since the
1930's. $b Lawrence and Lee began their collaboration working on
radio programs in the late 1930's, and gained fame with the Armed
Forces Radio Service (AFRS), which they helped to create in 1942.
While with the AFRS, they wrote a wide variety of programs that
were broadcast to troops overseas – comedy programs, dramatic
programs, and informational programs – including such titles as
Command Performance, Yarns for Yanks, and Mail Call.

545    $b After the war, Lawrence and Lee continued their
collaboration, working in commercial radio and producing such
programs as The Railroad Hour, Request Performance, Favorite
Story, and Young Love. At the same time, they began to write
musicals and television scripts, such as the television
adaptation of James Hilton's Lost Horizon, which was aired under
the title Shangri-La, and the musical production of Auntie Mame.
Overall, Lawrence and Lee produced many major works for radio,
television and stage.

FIGURE 1 (continued)

545    $b Both Lawrence and Lee have been active in more recent

years as teachers and lecturers, giving talks to a wide range of

academic and industry groups around the country and world.

520   The Lawrence and Lee collection includes a broad sample of

the material that this important team created for radio,

television, and the stage from the early 1940's into the 1960's.

$b Included in the collection are complete holdings for The

Railroad Hour, Favorite Story, and Young Love, as well as

representative holdings for Request Performance, Hallmark

Playhouse, A Date with Judy, and numerous other programs.

Holdings from their later activities include tapes of interviews

with and lectures given by one or both men, as well as private

recordings that document the development of scripts and stories

for Auntie Mame, Shangri-La, and The Gang's All Here.

520    $b All programs that Lawrence and Lee wrote or produced for

the Armed Forces Radio Service have been cataloged separately

under the heading of The Armed Forces Radio Service collection.

Cross references for these have been included in the Lawrence and

Lee local finding aid, but for more complete information about AFRS recordings by Lawrence and Lee, see the Armed Forces Radio Service local finding aid. Some of the AFRS programs that Lawrence and Lee worked on were: Command Performance, Mail Call, Yarns for Yanks, and Words with Music. Programs by Lawrence and Lee which were produced independently, and for which the archives has major holdings, have also been cataloged separately. These programs are: Favorite Story, and The Railroad Hour.

520   $b Material has been organized alphabetically by program title. All material pertaining to a given show - audition tapes, creative consultation tapes, reviews, etc. - have been collected under the show title.

561   Gift of Jerome Lawrence and Robert E. Lee.

506   Access to acetate discs restricted ; advance notification required.

555   Detailed finding aid available in repository. In: *L-Special 88-3.

650   0 Radio programs $x United States.

FIGURE 1 (continued)

```
700 10  Lee, Robert, $d 1918-
710 20  Armed Forces Radio Service.
730 01  Command performance, U.S.A. (Radio program)
730 01  Date with Judy (Radio program)
730 01  Favorite story.
730 01  Mail call (Radio program)
730 01  Railroad hour (Radio program)
730 01  Request performance (Radio program)
730 01  Words with music (Radio program)
730 01  Yarns for Yanks (Radio program)
730 01  Young love (Radio program)
851     $b Rodgers and Hammerstein Archives of Recorded Sound, $a New
York Public Library, $c 111 Amsterdam Ave., New York, NY 10023.
```

oration. Thus these recordings can and should be treated as an archival entity.

The title proper (field 245) in the example was created following *APPM* for title proper and dates.[3] It should be noted that archival practice recommends that collections gathered by an individual be entered under the title proper "Papers" — a term that would be misleading if it were to be used to describe a collection that is predominantly or completely sound recordings. Thus the term "Collection," a form term that implies less about the format of an archival entity, is frequently used for sound recordings collections even though it is generally prescribed for materials grouped "artificially around a person, subject, or activity and which otherwise lacks integrity and unity of provenance."[4]

Giving a sound recordings collection the title "Collection" by itself would be equally misleading, though, and so every title proper for collections of sound recordings should include an additional descriptive phrase or two. The title should be as specific as possible, without becoming unwieldy; other titles that might be used are: "Collection of radio broadcasts," or "Collection of piano performances." An example of a title not including the word "Collection" is "Selected speeches and addresses." It should be clear from this example that the General Material Designator (GMD) for archival sound recordings is crucial to give the user a clear sense of the physical nature of the collection.

The statement of physical extent in Figure 1 (field 300) follows *Anglo-American Cataloguing Rules (AACR2)*.[5] *APPM* further requires that a primary statement of extent be in linear or cubic feet, or in exact or approximate number of items. Since linear or cubic feet are not particularly helpful when describing the extent of a sound recordings collection, giving the extent in number of items is recommended. Because of the abundance of sound recordings formats, additional statements describing format-based subsets of a collection can be added if the archivist deems it necessary or useful. When this is done, the first statement should describe the collection in its entirety, and subsequent entries should describe the specific subsets. In all instances, MARC and *AACR2* standards are followed to construct the 300 in the correct form for sound recordings.

ORGANIZATION AND ARRANGEMENT

The concept of original order is of prime importance in archival work. Archivists attempt to use the original order of a collection as the basis of arrangement for a collection, under the assumption that this original order might contain evidential value to future researchers. The same holds for sound recordings, if the original order has been maintained. With sound recordings collections, however, original order is very rarely maintained by the people donating the collection, and can be very difficult to reconstruct. Almost all collections of sound recordings that arrive at an archives are boxed up in the most convenient packing method for the boxes used. If a given box filled with discs had a little more room to hold a few more things, and the only items that would fit were two tapes, then those tapes ended up in the box, regardless of their correct location. Thus the original order of a collection is often lost by the time the collection arrives at the archives.

When arranging a collection that has been scrambled, standard archival methods of arrangement can for the most part be followed. Arranging a sound recordings collection in chronological order or alphabetically by title is common, as is arranging a collection based on subject content. In the Lawrence and Lee collection, the series were based partly on a preliminary finding aid that was donated with the collection and partly on the subject contents of the remaining material. Frequently, collections arrive that are comprised partly of commercial and partly of noncommercial recordings. In these situations, R & H catalogers create separation lists for the commercial recordings that give the title, label name, and issue number for each recording. The commercial recordings are then processed separately. The organization and arrangement field (field 351) is used according to AMC specification.

Notes fields that are commonly used for sound recordings collections are for the most part the same as those used for textual archival collections. These include, in order of appearance in a record: biographical note (field 545), scope and contents (field 520), terms governing use and reproduction (field 540), and cumulative index/ finding aids note (field 555), among others. Whether these fields are included, and their length and complexity when they are included, must be determined by the cataloging institution. The restrictions on access note (field 506) is one example of a notes field that is used in slightly different form for sound recordings collections. With sound recordings collections, access restrictions might differ from format to format. For example, shellac test pressings are more stable than lacquer acetate discs, and might be given different access restrictions. These restrictions must be clearly explained in the catalog record. For instance, when the collection contains acetate and other disc recordings, such as vinyl or shellac discs:

- Access to acetate discs restricted; advance notification required.

When the collection contains only acetate disc recordings, along with other format sound recordings:

- Access to discs restricted; advance notification required.

When the collection consists entirely of acetate disc recordings:

- Access restricted; advance notification required.

FINDING AIDS

To archivists, the finding aid is a central tool for describing a collection and locating items in it, and is used to direct users to a subset of the collection for further work. With sound recordings archival entities, the finding aid is usually the *only* tool for access to any part of a collection. Whereas textual material can be brought to the user for further visual evaluation, sound recordings are not browsable, but must be heard to be evaluated. With print material, browsing is also possible because a user can page through three or four folders of letters, each holding 60 letters, or 200 items, and evaluate their importance. With sound recordings, there are physical restrictions: 200 sound recordings take up approximately two feet of shelf space and weigh almost 200 pounds. Even if the user could look at that many sound recordings, in most cases it wouldn't be possible to tell what is on the discs, since noncommercial discs often don't have any written information on them. Thus, for sound recordings, the finding aid is the sole method of access. For this reason, the finding aid for archival sound recordings should be as detailed as possible.

Another reason for providing highly detailed finding aids for archival sound recordings revolves around the needs and expectations that the users of sound recordings have. Sound recordings libraries have historically attempted to provide analytic access to their holdings. Cataloging for sound recordings thus includes a larger number of name and name/title added entries than most other cataloging. Users of recordings collections have come to expect this sort of access. Since archival sound recordings often contain material that will still be of interest to the usual user seeking recordings, the archivist should strive to provide this access.

Due to these circumstances, the finding aids created at R & H for archival sound recordings collections are usually at the item level. With the use of a local database manager, finding aids are generated with a main listing that is similar to a catalog card (see Figure 2). This level of detail affects the AMC cataloging because a finding aid of this complexity can lead to the inclusion of a large number of name added entries, since the finding aid is often used as the basis for determining added entries. *APPM* does not address the issue of performer added entries or analytical added entries, except to state that "if, in the context of a given catalog, added entries are required under headings and titles other than those prescribed . . . make them."[6]

Since analytic and performer added entries can be essential to the access of a sound recordings collection, R & H has adopted a policy of including as many of these name added entries as are known. As the finding aid is created, most of the authority work for the names is done, and adding them to the cataloging becomes a matter of keying in the names. Each added entry also includes a relator code (subfield 4) that specifies what action the person or group did in the collection. This follows standard sound recordings cataloging practice, but differs from archival cataloging practice. If an archives aims to give name access to its sound recordings collections at a detailed or analytic level, then these names should be added to the AMC entry, in the form that will be most useful to all users.

However, including analytical added entries for sound recordings

Figure 2: Sample entry from finding aid:

Lucky Strike presents: Your hit parade. 12-31-38.

8 sound discs : analog, 78 rpm, aluminum-based acetate ; 10 in.

Radio program.

Two different copies of part 9 and 11.

Contents incomplete.

Originals in *LJ-10 559, *LJ-10 560, *LJ-10 561, *LJ-10 562,
*LJ-10 563, *LJ-10 564, *LJ-10 565, *LJ-10 566.

Contents: What have you got that gets me? -- I won't tell a soul
-- This can't be love -- New Year's Eve in a haunted house --
My reverie -- You got me -- Once in a while -- Don't wait til
the night before Christmas -- All ashore -- The penguin --
Two sleepy people -- Deep in a dream of you -- There's a gold
mine in the sky -- Tango du reve -- Closing.

1. Ross, Lanny prf 2. The Raymond Scott Quintet prf

collections can yield extremely long AMC records. It is not uncommon for a moderately-sized collection to contain sixty or seventy performers, of which the added entries alone would take up almost a full screen; larger collections can have many more.[7] In an attempt to shorten these records, R & H has experimented with using relator codes and a general performer note to eliminate at least the double entry of each name required by *AACR2* rule 21.29.[8] By entering a note that states the role of performers in a general way and appending a relator code to each name, the record can be shortened greatly. A general note can also serve to alert the user to the great length of the record. This approach is a compromise; it is less clear than including a performer note that specifies each performer's role, and thus is only used in extreme instances.

SUBJECT INDEXING

Subject headings for most archival sound recordings collections tend to be form subject headings rather than topical. A sound recording of a symphony isn't about symphonies, but is one; thus the subject heading it receives reflects its form rather than its subject. This is largely true for archival sound recordings collections as well. The greater portion of subject headings that are assigned at R & H are form subject headings that are taken from the *Library of Congress Subject Headings* (*LCSH*).[9] The depth of indexing that is done can vary from institution to institution and from collection to collection depending on the needs of the users. At R & H, each collection will receive one or more subject headings for the entire collection. If the collection contains any series that in the judgment of the cataloger are especially important, then additional headings will be added for those more specific topics or forms. The emphasis, however, is on assigning headings for the collection, rather than for the individual items in it.

Determining appropriate headings for a sound recordings collection follows standard archival practice. Archival subject indexing for textual collections often relies on the contents of the finding aid to determine appropriate headings. The cataloger assigns headings by analyzing the finding aid, and analysis can be performed at the collection level, the series level, or even at the item level. This method can be used for sound recordings collections as well.

In addition, archival cataloging often assigns two additional types of terms to AMC records; one of these is the form-genre term, that gives a summary of the form or forms that a collection contains; the other is the occupation index term. The form-genre term is useful because archival users often look for information that comes in standardized forms, such as address books, diaries, or minutes; archivists add these terms to the bibliographic record to allow users to retrieve records for material by form. The terms are taken from various lists that have been compiled; R & H uses a list compiled by the Research Libraries Group,[10] although other lists are available. When these terms can be applied to a sound recordings collection, they should be added according to AMC specifications; the forms contained in a collection of sound recordings rarely correlate to the forms on the RLG list, so R & H has rarely used this part of a bibliographic record. An example of form-genre terms is given in Figure 3.

Related to form-genre terms are occupation terms, which identify occupations reflected in the contents of the described material. Occupation terms can be taken from a number of sources; *LCSH* is one such source. Headings for occupations that are included in *LCSH* can be used as occupation headings. Figure 3 includes an instance of an occupation term.

CONCLUSION

Cataloging archival sound recordings collections in many ways is similar to cataloging of textual archival collections. Sound recordings collections can be evaluated as to their archival value using the same criteria as textual materials: provenance, whether the material is published or noncommercial, and whether the material contains contextual value. A collection of sound recordings that fulfill these criteria can and should be treated as an archival entity, so as to preserve the collection's identity. AMC entries for sound recordings collections often have titles proper and statements of extent that differ somewhat from the cataloging for textual collections, and

Figure 3: Subject headings, form-genre terms, and occupations.

ID: NYPW87-A197 RTYP:d ST:s MS: EL: AD:09/24/87

CC: nyu BLT:bc DCF:a CSC:d MOD: PROC:p UD:04/12/88

PP:nyu L:eng PC:i PD:1942/1966 REP:?

MMD: OR: POL: DM: RR: COL: EML: GEN: BSE:

040 NN $c NN $e appm

245 00 Marian McPartland's piano jazz $h [sound recording], $f 197--

300 81 sound tapes : $b analog.

300 80 sound tapes : $b analog, 7 1/2 ips, 2 track, stereo. ; $c
10 in.

300 1 sound cassette : $b analog ; $c Dolby-processed.

500 Tape recordings made for broadcast on radio program of the
same title.

520 Weekly radio program in which host Marian McPartland
interviews guest musicians, usually famous jazz pianists, about
their careers and music. $b Each program is dedicated to one
guest performer who talks about his/her technique and style of
playing, and trades stories with McPartland in a casual

atmosphere. The show features the work of the guest player in live, solo piano performances, as well as in impromptu duets with McPartland.

520 $b Included in the collection are recordings (2 sound tape reels : analog, 7 1/2 ips, 2 track, stereo. ; 10 in. and 1 sound cassette) of the presentation event, which took place October 28, 1985 at the Bruno Walter Auditorium of The New York Public Library. Speakers: George Wein, Henry Cauthen, and Mariam McPartland. "Concert by Marian McPartland, George Shearing, and others." -- Presentation program.

500 Presentation event reels shelved in: *LT-10 4110 no. 79-80 ; cassette shelved in: *LTC 1253.

561 Gift of the South Carolina Educational Radio and TV Network, and Marian McPartland; 1985-1989.

500 List of programs available at Archives.

FIGURE 3 (continued)

650 0   Radio programs $z United States.

650 0   Jazz musicians $x Interviews.

650 0   Jazz piano.

650 0   Piano music (jazz)

656 7   Pianists. $2 lcsh

655 7   Sound recordings. $2 ftamc

655 7   Interviews. $2 ftamc

700 10 McPartland, Marian.

730 01 Piano jazz (radio program)

851     $b Rodgers and Hammerstein Archives of Recorded Sound, $a New
        York Public Library, $c 111 Amsterdam Ave., New York, NY 10023,

care must be used when creating these fields to ensure that users of the catalog can clearly identify the nature of the collection.

Sound recordings collections can be arranged following standard archival practice. Chronological, alphabetical, and subject-based arrangements work well for sound recordings, just as they do for textual collections. Because sound recordings collections can't really be browsed, finding aids and bibliographic records must if possible be more detailed, so that portions of a collection may be located accurately. The abundance of performers in a sound recordings collection, and the importance that those performers have to the user of sound recordings can result in a larger number of name added entries than most bibliographic records have. Finally, subject headings for archival sound recordings collections tend to be form headings, and can be assigned following usual practices.

Because of the similarities that the cataloging processes for textual and recorded archival collections have, the bibliographic record for an archival sound recordings collection will be very similar to the record for a textual collection, except that it will usually be much longer, and contain many more added entries than the entry for a textual collection. This results from the fact that archival sound recordings collections must try to meet the needs of two very distinct audiences: the sound recordings library user, and the sound recordings archive user. These users usually expect different modes of access—modes that are often opposed. The library user often looks for information contained within specific works or items, while the archival user often looks for information contained in the relationship between specific works or items. The different needs of these user groups has been served in the past with two opposed cataloging practices, which must now be blended by the sound recordings cataloger. With care, however, a sound recordings cataloger or archivist can preserve both types of information, and thus serve both types of user.

NOTES

1. Steven Hensen. *Archives, Personal Papers and Manuscripts* (2nd. ed. Draft, 1989), p. 8.

2. ". . . collections of manuscripts and archival records are usually formed

around a person, family group or corporate body, based on provenance, and contain material generated by or addressed to the person, family, or corporate body.'' Hensen, *Archives*, p. 5.

3. Hensen, *Archives*, pp. 11-14.

4. Hensen, *Archives*, p. 12.

5. *Anglo-American Cataloguing Rules*. Second edition, 1988 revision. (Chicago: American Library Association, 1988).

6. Hensen, *Archives*, p. 43.

7. In one instance at R & H, an important collection (the Lauder Greenway Opera and Recital Collection, 1901-1971) of almost 700 opera recordings listed over 500 singers, each of whom received an added entry. Online, the added entries alone for this record take up nearly 10 screens.

8. ''If the reason for an added entry is not apparent from the description . . . provide a note giving, as appropriate, the name of the person or body (see 1.7B6) and/or the title (see 1.7B4).'' *AACR2*, p. 355.

9. *Library of Congress Subject Headings*. 12th ed. (Washington, D.C.: Cataloging Distribution Service, 1989).

10. *Form Terms for Archival and Manuscripts Control*. ([Stanford, Calif.]: Research Libraries Group, 1985).

Control of Cartographic Materials in Archives

James Corsaro

SUMMARY. Archival repositories are a major source of cartographic information useful for many kinds of research. Access to
these cartographic resources is an integral part of their availability
and is related to the general principles of archival arrangement and
description. The automation of archival access using the MARC
Format for Archives and Manuscripts Control has created great
changes in archival description practices. Although there has been a
MARC Format for Maps for several years, this format is not as
useful for the description of cartographic archives and archivists
have not yet developed the generally accepted standards needed to
make these materials accessible to a wide range of users. This paper
discusses the differences in archival and bibliographic description of
maps and suggests some possible options for standards development
in the control of cartographic archives.

Cartographic materials are found in most archival and manuscript
repositories and are an indispensable research resource for a variety
of users. Land planners, environmentalists, historic preservation-
ists, surveyors, genealogists, historians, lawyers, geologists and
legislative policymakers all find the unique descriptive information
of maps and atlases vital for successful research. These resources
often provide information not found in textual records, and are useful for verifying the existence and change over time of natural and
manmade features in an environment. For instance, the location of a
particular landholding, transportation routes, industrial sites or increasingly potential toxic waste dumps can frequently be verified by

James Corsaro is Associate Librarian, Manuscripts and Special Collections,
New York State Library, Albany, NY.

examining maps. In sum, cartographic collections provide significant insights and information about the physical and cultural context in which human activities take place.

In recognition of the importance of cartographic materials libraries have cataloged printed maps and atlases for many years. Standard rules for cataloging printed maps exist and a MARC Format for Maps has been used since 1971. The literature of map librarianship repeatedly indicates the necessity for bibliographic control of map collections. Indeed, the standard manual of map librarianship states that a library must make its map collections accessible and the "best way to do that is by having the entire collection cataloged and on the general library database — cataloging time saved once is reference time spent over and over."[1] The unfortunate reality is that surprisingly few libraries actually catalog maps considering the potential for copy cataloging available for printed maps.[2] Maps constitute less than .4% of the RLIN database (164,395 map records of a total count of 37,828,663 bibliographic records). In addition, the vast majority of maps cataloged on RLIN and OCLC appear to have been published in the last twenty years. In addition, there is a very low percentage of historical maps described in the national online bibliographic databases. Archival map records are also few and far between; in the RLIN AMC File only 2363 records of 236,395 records, about 1%, identify maps as all or part of a series or collection.[3]

The library profession has at least articulated a set of standards and cataloging rules for making maps accessible through local catalogs and national online bibliographic databases, even if only some libraries follow the standards.[4] The archival profession is in a good deal worse state, however. It is the thesis of this essay that standard provisions for controlling maps in archives are only sketched out in general terms and there is a need for generally accepted guidelines and procedures. The cataloging practices for maps developed by the library profession are not completely applicable for providing access to maps found in an archival context. Library cataloging of maps is chiefly item-directed and concentrates on the physical characteristics of maps, whereas archival maps require a greater emphasis on the context in which the maps were created and their intellectual content characteristics. Archival maps pose special problems because of their uniqueness and often very fragile physical condition, and the large number of maps in specific archival series may make item description a difficult, and often impossible task as well.

THE NEED FOR STANDARDS
FOR CARTOGRAPHIC ARCHIVES

The literature of cartographic archives is small and consists chiefly of journal articles and chapters in various manuals of archival practice, most describing National Archives practice, which is not necessarily typical of many repositories.[5] These quite often mention the importance of treating maps in terms of their archival context, but then instruct the reader in library methods of bibliographic control. One archival text is devoted to cartographic archives. Ralph Ehrenberg's *Archives and Manuscripts: Maps and Architectural Drawings* provides useful information about the arrangement and description of maps within archives, but includes only one paragraph about the conversion of map cataloging to machine readable format and refers to two Library of Congress manuals on the MARC format, neither dealing with archival maps and both somewhat outdated.[6] This manual defines two categories of archival maps: those part of textual files and those created as separate files.[7] Actually four categories of archival maps may be differentiated, each needing somewhat different guidelines or standards. These categories include: single items, for example a manuscript map of the Ohio River dated 1795; map collections brought together by a collector, geographer, scientist or other person, such as the James Hall Geological Map Collection; map series created by a government or business as part of their daily operations, such as cadastral maps of the Little Nine Partners Patent; and textual records including maps, such as the Van Rensselaer Manor Papers, which include surveys and maps.

As part of the preparation for a grant application to the National Historical Publications and Records Commission (NHPRC), a telephone survey of ten institutions with substantial map collections was conducted. The survey included the Library of Congress, the National Archives, university libraries and archives, and historical societies that hold state archival records.[8] The survey requested information about cataloging practices and manuals in use, whether their cartographic holdings are cataloged in MARC Maps or Archives and Manuscripts files in automated systems, what subject authorities are used, and how description and physical arrangement were linked. The survey found that none of the institutions had manuals or forms which could be used anywhere but in their institution; few use the AMC file in RLIN, but instead catalog maps in the MAPS file because of their perception that maps are single bibliographic items rather than parts of archival series and all stated that they had either poor or non-existent subject access to their maps.

In addition, there are no descriptive standards for cataloging archival maps in online databases. The Archival and Manuscripts Control format (AMC) is useful for cataloging archival series and collections, but does not include some important data elements for maps, such as scale, projection, engraver or lithographer, and geographic area code. For instance, there are many bibliographic records for maps in the AMC file of RLIN which are described as "Maps and Atlases" or "Map Collection" with little further description, essentially telling the user nothing about the unique map-related characteristics of the series. Archivists have no guidelines for determining the appropriate file in which to catalog maps; the MAPS file or AMC file of RLIN, for instance. Nor are there any standards for determining when to describe archival maps as series or as single items. In summary, there are no generally accepted standards that archivists can use in dealing with their archival map collections.

ARCHIVAL DESCRIPTION OF MAPS

What makes an archival map different from a map found in a library collection? Libraries generally treat maps as single bibliographic entities with an emphasis on the physical description of the map and its contents. Thus, the size of the map, the scale and projection at which it is drawn as well as the more typically book-oriented data elements such as title, author and subjects are considered when cataloging. The context in which the map was created is of no importance in its cataloging.

Maps found in archival collections or series differ because the context of their creation is central to understanding their meaning and significance. Archival records are the creation and result of the routine activities of an organization, business, governmental body or individual and thereby represent the what, how, when and why of these activities. The context in which these activities are conducted gives them meaning and helps to explain the records created by the activities. It is a central principle of archival work that the "respect des fonds" and provenance are always maintained, that is the records are kept together in their original order according to their organic relationship to the creator's activity and function.[9] For instance, the papers of a novelist might include manuscripts of books, correspondence and contracts with publishers. The letters might include references to the novels, and the novels might include incidents or characters mentioned in the letters. The collection as a whole is therefore greater than the sum of its parts and the provenance or link between the novelist and the papers is essential to understanding it.

Maps, as parts of archival collections, have the same characteristics as textual records. For instance, a map found in the records of a state commission to investigate "subversive activities" in New York State in 1919, shows the meeting places of supposed radical or subversive groups. Upon examination of the commission records, one finds minutes of hearings and testimony that mention these meeting places and describe the "subversive activities" that occured there. The minutes provide meaning and significance to the map and vice-versa.[10]

When a map collector, geographer, or scientist over a lifetime creates a collection of maps of a particular locality or of a particular period of time such as the American Revolution, the collection represents both the subjects and the collector's taste and knowledge. Archival description also records information about the condition and things that have been done to archival material, so if the geographer or collector annotated, preserved, framed or carried out other actions on the maps these would be noted in the description also.

Lastly, if a large landowner leases or sells lands over a long period of time and determines that there is a necessity to map the leased or sold lands, the resulting maps and perhaps textual material associated with them such as surveys, leases, contracts and so forth become important in representing the history of that land. These cadastral maps depict the functions and activities of the landowner and surveyor as well as the responsibilities of the lessee or buyer of the land, and are therefore necessary to an understanding of their history.

When describing such records with the purpose of making them as accessible as possible, it is necessary to describe these links between the creator of the archives and the archives themselves. Referring to the above example of cadastral maps, one can hypothesize a situation in which a search is conducted for a large group of such maps, as well as surveyors' notes, leases, rent records and so forth from the late 18th century. A modern land developer would like to place a subdivision on the mapped land, but must first satisfy various environmental regulations concerning the potential historical or archeological significance of the land. A major source for the research would be the archives of this landowner, and access to the records is very important. If the maps were cataloged singly by library map cataloging rules, there would not necessarily be any reference to the additional material, which is related to the maps and provides the context of their creation. In archival description it is required that such contextual description occur and so the developer's archeologist should be able to find all the pertinent material.

There are some additional considerations for describing archival maps. Archival maps are often unique manuscript maps or printed maps with manuscript annotations. This as well as the frequent fragile condition of historical maps produces preservation and access concerns. Since it is important that these unique maps be preserved it might be necessary to file them separately from the main series of which they are a part. However, it is equally important that the cataloging of the maps reflects their intimate connection with the series. Because archival maps are often manuscript drawings or sketches, the typical elements found on printed maps (such as projection, scale, date, author, complete title, and so forth) might not be present. The series context of these maps is especially important in these cases because it might provide the only source of information for these data elements of the maps.

Some archival series contain hundreds, perhaps thousands of individual maps. Unlike printed map series, such as the U. S. Geological Survey topographic map series, these maps are not uniform in scale, size and geographic region or subject matter. It is likely that each map will be unique in one or another aspect. While it would be good to have a bibliographic entry for each of these unique maps as well as the series description, the reality is that most archival repositories have backlogs of descriptive work and will not have an opportunity to create individual cataloging for perhaps hundreds of maps. Series description is a necessity in such situations.

REQUIREMENTS FOR CARTOGRAPHIC ARCHIVAL STANDARDS

These unique characteristics of archival maps require a different group of options for their description in order to provide the most appropriate and complete access. What are some of these possibilities? Before mentioning some options, it should be reiterated that there is no uniform agreement on standards for archival description of maps. The NHPRC grant referred to above is directed at this need and one of the goals of the project is the definition and proposal of such guidelines and standards. The project will address issues concerning standards about whether to catalog maps as single bibliographic entities or as archival series, and when both processes might be necessary. Standards are also needed to assist archivists to describe maps that are parts of series with textual or visual formats; the appropriate bibliographic file, MAPS or AMC, to use for various categories of maps or map series, and whether different data elements or cataloging practices will be necessary for printed and manuscript maps.

A sample record might be helpful in displaying these standards concerns. A state geologic survey is a typical government agency involved in the creation of numerous maps, both working copies and final products. Figure 1 indicates some of the typical data elements found in an archival map collection cataloged in the AMC format. Map librarians will no doubt note the absence of any mention of *individual* map titles, authors, and physical description. Mention of specific geographic coverage is also absent, and there is no field for mathematical data. Librarians might question the lack of this information. Such questions are valid and need to be ad-

Figure 1

110   $aNew York (State). $b Division of Science and State Museum.

245   $aGeologic maps and drawings, $f 1842-1971

300   $aca. 6 cu. ft. $f (ca. 500 maps/drawings)

351   $b Portions in chronological order

520   $aThis series consists of working, proof, and final published copies of
      geologic maps and drawings prepared by the Geological Survey staff in
      the State Museum. $b(here the entry describes the series in greater
      detail.)

541   $aSeries was transferred to the Archives by the Geological Survey in
      1979....

555   $aList of individual maps or groups of maps in each folder or roll

580   $aAgency record NYSV86-a826 describes the history and functions of the
      New York State Museum

851   $aNew York State $bArchives, $cCultural Education Center, Albany, N.Y.

dressed by archivists as part of the development of descriptive standards. It is equally important that the standards of archival description are not lost in attempting to make these archival map records like library map entries.

Figures 2 and 3 exhibit the same map cataloged in the AMC Format and in the MAPS Format. The AMC entry does not include: (1) a Library of Congress Classification Number field (050) since archival records are not classified; (2) a Mathematical Data field (255) since scale is currently not available for use in an AMC record; or, (3) an Imprint field (260) since publication information is not usually relevant in AMC records and so is rarely noted. Perhaps more significant, the title entry for the AMC Format record differs considerably from the MAPS Format entry. In archival description the Title Statement field (245) is to be used for creation of a descriptive title rather than a straight-forward transcription of a title from the map itself. The Added Entry: Variant Title field, Added Entry-Variant Title has been used for the transcription of titles found on the map. This discrepancy is an issue that should be addressed in the development of descriptive standards for archival maps. Two fields, Scope and Content Note (520) and Historical/Biographical Note (545), found in the AMC record are absent in the MAPS record. These fields describe the history of the committee whose activities created the map (545), and secondly, present information about the map itself, which in a map record would be a briefer 500 General Note field. Two other fields found on the AMC record not found on a MAPS form are the Form/Genre index term (655) and the Location field (851). Form/genre terms, in this case referenced from the *Art and Architecture Thesaurus (AAT)* indicate functionally specific or stylistically or technically distinguishable terms, useful for archival research because they explain something about the functions and activities of the creator of the material. The Location field (851) contrasts with the 850 Holdings field in that it provides a full address of the location of the material. Since archival material is unique it is important to indicate the exact address of its location, as contrasted with published material for which a brief NUC entry in the Holdings field is usually adequate. Lastly, the Linking Entry Complexity Note field (580) and Host Item Entry field (773) in the AMC record indicate that the map is part of a

Figure 2

035    $aA3285

110    $aNew York (State). $bJoint Legislative Committee to Investigate
       Seditious Activities.

245    $aNew York City map of locations of ethnic radicals' meeting
       places and newspaper publishers, $f1919.

545    $aThe Joint Legislative Committee to Investigate Seditious
       Activities was established in 1917 to investigate individuals and
       groups suspected of radical activities to overthrow the State and
       Federal government.   Committee staff attended meetings and
       infiltrated suspected radical organizations.   The Committee
       completed its investigation and published a lengthy report in
       1920.

520

$aThis map was annotated by the Attorney General's Office for use by the Joint Committee to assist in identifying potential organizations and neighborhoods to investigate. $bThe map uses color coding to identify areas populated by the following ethnic groups suspected of radical activity: Germans; Russian Jews; Italians; Austro-Hungarians; Irish; Chinese; Scandanavian and Finns; Syrians, Turks, Armenians, and Greeks; French; and Negroes. The map also uses a number code to identify buildings in Manhattan and the Bronx where meetings of suspected radicals were held. Also identified by a separate number code are the locations of "radical and liberal" newspapers and periodicals published in New York City.

FIGURE 2 (continued)

580    $aForms part of: Joint Legislative Committee to Investigate Seditious Activities. Investigative files of radical organizations, 1917-1919.

655    $aMaps$2aat

740    $aEthnic map

773    $w(CStRLIN)NYSV86-A144

851    $aNew York State Archives and Records Administration, Albany, New York

Figure 3

034 $b16800

050 $aG3804.N4:2M3 1917

052 3804 $bN4:2M3

110 $aNew York (State).$bJoint Legislative Committee Investigating
    Seditious Activities.

245 $aEthnic map prepared under the direction of John B. Trevor by Clarence
    L. Converse

255 $aScale [1:16,800]

260 $aNew York, N.Y. $bA.R. Ohman $c[1917]

300 $a1 map $bcol.; $c119 × 46 cm.

500 $aManuscript notations and colors keyed to indicate various ethnic
    groups.

500 $aDrawn upon New Quick Reference Street Indexed Map of the Borough of
    Manhattan.

500 $aIndexes to radical meeting halls and radical and liberal newspapers.

larger archival collection, and reference the collection number for further information. This example, though somewhat simplified and reduced in length, serves to illustrate the contrasts between the use of various fields in the AMC and MAPS Formats. Anyone interested in developing standards of bibliographic description for archival maps in automated systems will necessarily have to address these contrasts and issues.

Some of the issues might, of course, be solved by the advent of format integration in 1992. Integrating the various formats will allow catalogers and archival processors to use essentially all of the MARC fields. Imagine an AMC map record that includes a scale statement and a specific physical description field, as well as an historical note and scope and content note. Whether such an AMC record might be possible or desirable is an issue that must be considered. This will not exempt archivists from choosing the appropriate file, AMC or MAPS, for their records, but it will allow them greater flexibility in perhaps choosing to add the record to both files or to reference the record from one file to another.

CONCLUSION

The advent of the MARC AMC Format for archives has provided a vehicle for archivists to begin to communicate through automated bibliographic systems and it now provides greatly increased access opportunities for researchers nationally. However, this newfound strength comes with some responsibilities as well. It has become imperative that archivists develop descriptive standards and bibliographic control mechanisms that allow them to communicate efficiently and accurately. Since maps are an integral part of nearly all archival repositories, there is a need for clear and appropriate standards for this format. One of the most important facets of this work towards standards is that it addresses "the specific description of a particular type of archival material that is physically and logically within a larger group of archival records of various formats . . . the techniques . . . for maps will also define a conceptual framework within which procedures for other types of specialized materials could also be dealt with."[11] Increased standardization of communication will allow a greater integration of all of a library's or archives' access tools thereby providing better information for researchers, the ultimate purpose of all our work.

NOTES

1. Larsgaard, Mary Lynette, *Map Librarianship: An Introduction*, 2nd ed., Littleton, CO.: Libraries Unlimited, Inc., 1987, p. 162.

2. Cobb, David, *Bulletin of the Geography and Map Division, Special Libraries Association*, June 1988. Statistics quoted by Cobb at an IFLA meeting found that the OCLC map database contained 186,000 records, of which the Library of Congress added 110,000 and all other U. S. libraries only 75,000 records.

3. Search of the RLIN database, January 1990; bibliographic total includes all the major files: Archives and Manuscripts Control, Books, Map, Recordings, Scores, Serials, Visual Materials, and Machine Readable Data Files.

4. Cartmell, Vivian and Velma Parker, *Cartographic Materials: A Manual of Interpretation for AACR2*, Chicago, American Library Association, 1982; OCLC, *Maps Format*, Columbus, Ohio, 1986; Carrington, David K. and Elizabeth U. Mangan, *Data Preparation Manual for the Conversion of Map Cataloging Records to Machine-Readable Form*, Washington: Library of Congress 1971; Rescarch Libraries Group, *RLIN Supplement to USMARC Bibliographic Format*, Stanford, CA: RLG, 1989.

5. Friss, Herman R. "Cartographic and Related Records: What are they, How have they been produced and What are problems of their administration?" *American Archivist*, April 1950: 135-155; Joerg, W.L.G., "Archival Maps as illustrated by those in the National Archives" *American Archivist*, July 1941: 188-193; Schellenberg, Theodore R., "Arrangement and Description of Cartographic Records" in *The Management of Archives*, New York: Columbia University Press, 1965: 302-321.

6. Ehrenberg, Ralph, *Archives and Manuscripts: Maps and Architectural Drawings*, Chicago, Society of American Archivists, 1982. Ehrenberg's manual is the only generally useful manual available for archivists dealing with cartographic materials. It discusses all aspects of archival management of cartographic records.

7. Ibid, p. 42.

8. The Alabama Department of Archives and History, the New York State Library, Manuscripts and Special Collections Unit, and the New York State Archives and Records Administration have received a grant from the National Historical Publications and Records Commission to develop guidelines for describing their archival map holdings. The survey was conducted in 1989 and included besides those mentioned in the text, Bentley Historical Library, Georgia Department of Archives and History, Louisiana State University Special Collections, Mississippi Department of Archives and History, Minnesota Historical Society, New York Public Library Rare Books and Manuscripts, State Historical Society of Wisconsin, Yale University Department of Manuscripts and Archives.

9. Further information about the principles of provenance and of original order can be found in Schellenber, p. 41-45; Pederson, Ann, *Keeping Archives*, Sydney: Australian Society of Archivists, Inc., p. 116-117, and other texts on archival theory.

10. Records of the New York State Joint Legislative Committee to Investigate Seditious Activities, New York State Archives and Records Administration, Cultural Education Center, Albany, New York.

11. NHPRC Grant Application Support Letter from Richard V. Szary, May 10, 1989.